More True Tales of the Paranormal

More True Tales of the Paranormal

Ghosts, Poltergeists, Near-Death Experiences, and other Mysterious Events

Kimberly Molto, PhD

DUNDURN PRESS
TORONTO

Edited by Tony Hawke
Copy-edited by Phon Baillie
Designed by Courtney Horner
Printed and bound in Canada by Webcom

Library and Archives Canada Cataloguing in Publication

Molto, Kimberly
    More true tales of the paranormal : ghosts, poltergeists, near-death experiences, and other mysterious events / Kimberly Molto.

ISBN 978-1-55002-834-8

    1. Parapsychology. 2. Parapsychology and science. I. Title.

BF1031.M63 2008   133   C2008-903941-6

1 2 3 4 5   12 11 10 09 08

We acknowledge the support of **The Canada Council for the Arts** and the **Ontario Arts Council** for our publishing program. We also acknowledge the financial support of the **Government of Canada** through the **Book Publishing Industry Development Program** and **The Association for the Export of Canadian Books**, and the **Government of Ontario** through the **Ontario Book Publishers Tax Credit** program, and the **Ontario Media Development Corporation**.

Care has been taken to trace the ownership of copyright material used in this book. The author and the publisher welcome any information enabling them to rectify any references or credits in subsequent editions.

J. Kirk Howard, President

Printed and bound in Canada.
Printed on recycled paper.
www.dundurn.com

Dundurn Press
3 Church Street, Suite 500
Toronto, Ontario, Canada
M5E 1M2

Gazelle Book Services Limited
White Cross Mills
High Town, Lancaster, England
LA1 4XS

Dundurn Press
2250 Military Road
Tonawanda, NY
U.S.A. 14150

This book is dedicated with love to Terrance Clayton and in loving memory of my father, Gordon Molto, brother Gary Molto, and in honour of Dr. Viktor E. Frankl.

Contents

Preface
Crossing the Rubicon

Even though I thought I might want to take a break from writing with all the research, interviews, transcribing and field investigations that went into my first book, *True Tales of the Paranormal: Hauntings, Poltergeists, Near Death Experiences, and other Mysterious Events,* before the final edits were even done, unseen influences already had the second book in motion. I was caught in the currents of the river Rubicon. For those

Author reflected on tombstone during field investigation.

not familiar with that reference, I had intended to call that first book "Rubicon," referring to Caesar, who had his armies massed on the banks of the river Rubicon. Crossing it would be tantamount to a declaration of war and once done, there would be no turning back, or as Caesar himself put it, *"Alea iacta est,"* the die has been cast. Experiences with the paranormal have that same effect on the lives of those these things happen to. You are never the same, you do not see life and death in the same way and there is no turning back or away from it. I refer to it as a Rubicon event. For the majority of people, this is a very good, life-altering experience that broadens their minds, alters their perceptions, and re-arranges their priorities in life. My plans for a break were not to be. I again found myself caught in the currents of the Rubicon, only this time I found the water to be steely blue and icy cold. The kind of cold that really wakes you up, either freezing you to death or enlightening you. As with the first book, I did not feel I had a choice in the matter. There had been a close succession of deaths in my life of people very near and dear to me and I myself was experiencing the return of a lot of psychic activity. It may be purely whimsical on my part, but it felt like there were two opposing forces while writing this book. One attempting to hinder it, the other pushing and dragging me on. There were unseen influences, both internal and external. One of the external influences was the reaction I had received from people as a result of the first book. They said it had inspired them, made them feel less crazy and less alone; in fact, more connected. Their experiences made sense to them now. I also heard from people wanting to share their experiences and the effect it had on their lives even though they had never told another soul before, but were in hopes that it may help others.

What drew me so quickly into the second book were some unexpected events. The first was the re-emergence of an old friend, Marc Duffy, from high school who, having read *True Tales ...* was very inspired — especially with the chapter recounting the experiences of a young man who had died and was revived. Out of the blue, I received a call from Marc saying that he really needed to speak with me. He himself had died, was revived and had remained in a deep coma for several months. He didn't speak of it much at the time because it was the result of an attempted suicide drug overdose and he thought people would just think he was hallucinating. The other reason for his silence was that suicide was (and still is) a taboo subject and he feared people would just brush him off as a psychiatric case. After reading that chapter, he was finally ready to tell his story.

He also felt that sharing his experience may be of benefit to others, which is a common refrain from many of those I interviewed (they certainly were not coming forth for the attention!).

The other event was two messages I received from two psychics who had never met me before informing me (or each other, for that matter) that I would hear from a "Chris" and a "Ron," the latter being associated with the colour yellow. This intrigued me as I was already experiencing some strange events (and not for the first time) that I suspected were being generated by Ron. It turned out I was correct in my suspicions. The Ron the psychics were referring to was the husband of my older sister and a long-time close friend of mine. He owned a *yellow* Camaro that he absolutely loved. One evening while driving back from a music contest that my sister had won, they were hit head-on by a drunk driver. My sister, Sharlene, was thrown out the back window of their Volkswagen Beetle, dying instantly. Ron was also thrown from the car, and being unaware of her fate, crawled back to the car to save her. No sooner had he reached the car when it exploded in flames, which consumed him. Although I have never had contact with my sister, I have had contact with Ron. Sharlene knew from a young age that she was going to die young. Ron never had such a feeling and was not prepared to lose not only his life but his new wife, as well, and all the hopes and dreams they had. He did not die in peace. He felt he failed to save my sister and also died with hatred and resentment in his psyche toward my mother's firstborn son for his unrelenting interference in their marriage. (Never go to bed angry and try not to die with unresolved issues or hatred in your heart.) Sharlene was a talented poet and by yet another "coincidence" some of her poems came into my possession just this very year. One of them is a haunting poem that concludes Chapter 1. We have discerned that Ron's re-appearance is due to "unfinished business," which holds many spirits back. If he was unable to save her life, he could at least do his best to ensure that a part of her live on and be known by others because that poem being published. What is most poignant is that Chapter 1 is centred around a haunted house on Merion Street, and the poem was written when my family resided in a haunted house on that same street. We only die in the physical sense; our energy lives on in a different form. Apparently, love and dedication live on as well. I pray the publication of this thought-provoking poem brings some peace to my dear friend Ron.

The Chris the psychics were referring to was Chris Howard, who from the earliest of years was plagued by the interrelated and rare phenomena known as telekinesis and poltergeists. He declined to be interviewed for the first book, but, after reading it, agreed to an interview because he found it "enlightening and written in a non-sensational manner." Since he perceived that people had only benefited in one way or another, and no one in the book was pursued by the press or ridiculed by friends and family, he, like many of others, felt that perhaps sharing his story could be beneficial (Chris had a bad history with the press and researchers in the past). I am thrilled that Chris's experiences and insights are included in this book.

One of my most compelling reasons for writing the second book was that there was so much more to say and share; more unfinished business. Ironically, my background is in cognitive neurobiology and the consciousness. I had never envisioned myself writing a book on the paranormal, let alone two. The first book was difficult enough, beset with so many inexplicable events that I did not think I would ever get finished. The same occurred while producing this manuscript but as with the first book, I felt I had no choice in the matter. Maybe that's what happens when you are writing a book about "spooky" things. I am being facetious here as neither are spooky books. They are quite serious in nature, especially in the insights they have to offer us into the nature of life, death, and even reality.

Having a scientific background, I have always endeavoured to remain open-minded while maintaining a healthy dose of skepticism. To be an absolute believer in everything you hear about or an absolute denier teaches us nothing. Extremism in anything is never a good thing. Sometimes there are logical explanations for what first appears as an anomalous event. We must be open to and accept that. Not all pictures that have ORBs* in them are of ghosts. Nor are all voices that are heard on audio tape messages from the deceased. On the other hand, sometimes they are just that. So-called hard, serious science has been reluctant to delve into these mysterious events for various reasons, but even they are looking into it more seriously now. It is human nature to fear the unknown or face things that we cannot control or explain. We like to feel in control and be able to wrap things up with tidy explanations. However, life does not conform to what we would like. Things happen that we do not understand and cannot control. They only appear illogical because we don't understand them *yet*. As someone so aptly put it in this book, "We fear death and the unknown but what is the unknown? It is those things we just don't know or have not learnt yet." There was a time we didn't know anything about gravity or subatomic particles. In fact, any scientist who spoke of such things would be ridiculed, if not worse, but now we know and to deny the existence of these basic principles would result in ridicule. Some scientists may never come around. As Russell Targ and Harold Puthoff (both who research the paranormal) commented, one "serious" scientist responded to one of their papers by saying, "This is the kind of thing that I would not believe in even if it existed." This stands in stark contrast to such great scientific minds such as Albert Einstein who, though not a big proponent of the paranormal said, "The most beautiful thing we can experience is the mysterious. It is the source of all true art and all science. He to whom this emotion is a stranger, who can no longer pause to wonder and stand in rapt awe, is as good as dead; his eyes are closed." To such a scientist, I would remind them of the ancient Latin admonishment, *Aut disce aut discede,* either learn or leave." The more important point beyond what science thinks and what cannot be denied or debated is the effect these experiences have on the lives of those who have experienced them. As with my first book, I have presented a collection of extraordinary experiences that have happened to ordinary people. They are truly life-altering experiences. As I stress throughout the book, these experiences change our views of life and death, as well

* Purportedly, an indication of a ghostly presence, whether it is the spirit itself or spirit activity. See glossary for more details.

as their meaning and purpose, which is so vital because we are here for such a short time — some of us shorter than others. Whether you have or have not had such experiences or are just interested in the subject (perhaps you are wondering if there is more to life than meets the eye), I can only leave you with yet another Latin phrase and a parable about what our real priorities should be: *Aude sapere*: Dare to know. If you have had or will have such an experience, don't be afraid, don't think you are crazy, keep an open mind and learn from it. Remember, it happens to more people than you would suspect, from all walks of life and, I might add, that you are in very good company! For those who have had such experiences and wish to share them with others, I would be honoured to hear from you via the publisher or at drmolto@yahoo.ca. May your journey through this life be a meaningful and purposeful one.

———

A philosophy professor stood before his class and had some items in front of him. When the class began, wordlessly he picked up a large empty mayonnaise jar and proceeded to fill it with rocks, rocks about two inches in diameter. He then asked the students if the jar was full. They agreed that it was. So the professor then picked up a box of pebbles and poured them into the jar. He shook the jar lightly. The pebbles, of course, rolled into the open areas between the rocks. He then asked the students again if the jar was full. They agreed it was. The students laughed. The professor picked up a box of sand and poured it into the jar. Of course, the sand filled up everything else. "Now," said the professor, "I want you to recognize that this is your life. The rocks are the important things — your family, your partner, your health, your children — things that if everything else was lost and they only remained, your life would still be full. The pebbles are other things that matter like your job, your house, your car. The sand is everything else. The small stuff. If you put the sand into the jar first, there is no room for the pebbles or the rocks. The same goes for your life. If you spend all your time and energy on the small stuff, you will never have room for the things that are important to you. Pay attention to the things that are critical to your happiness. Play with your children. Take the time to get medical checkups. Take your partner out dancing. There will always be time to go to work, clean the house, give a dinner party and fix the disposal. Take care of the rocks first — the things that really matter. Set your priorities. The rest is just sand."

~ author unknown

Acknowledgements

The author wishes to thank Madeline Kinney, Julian Howard, Ian Godfrey, Dr. Michelle Douglas, Dr. Eric Howard, Michael Duffy, Chris Howard, Detective Tony Fenaro, and the rest of the team; Tony Hawke and those at Dundurn Press, Dale Kaczmarek of the Ghost Research Society, Matthew Didier of the Toronto Ghosts and Hauntings Research Society at torontoghosts.org, Jeff Belanger at ghostvillage.com, Guelph Public Library for their invaluable resources; Bill and Heather Vandivier, Ruth Anne Roth Clayton, Monique Skinner, RN (EC) NP-PHC, Tony Arpa who was across the way when it all began and remains still, and special thanks to all those people who generously shared their very personal stories in hopes that it would provide insight and comfort to others.

chapter 1
Merion Street Revisited:
You Can Go Home Again

Although I endeavour to write each account in an objective and professional manner, this chapter has a personal element to it. My journey through the paranormal, and personal crossing of the Rubicon was launched full speed when my family and I moved to a house on Merion Street. Thus, the title of the chapter, for although the protagonists of this narrative were moving into what was for them a brand new home, for me it was like coming home. While it may be literally true that we can never go home again, we can sure visit the old neighbourhood! Besides, I don't think we ever really leave home. We carry pieces of it around in us for the rest of our lives.

———

Ian Godfrey has been a good friend of mine since the mid 1970s. We have kept in touch over the years and have even worked together on a couple of projects. In fact, one of those projects was my first book, *True Tales of the Paranormal.* The first chapter of that book was about the experiences my family and I had had in a house on 13 Merion Street in Guelph, Ontario. You can imagine my reaction when Ian called to ask me if I could help he and his longtime girlfriend with their moving "project," going on to say that they were moving from their condominium in nearby Kitchener to a house on Merion Street! This

Photo by Kimberly Molto

Merion Street. One of the most psychically active cells in Guelph — also known as a "hot zone."

street is a very pleasant, quiet street lined with trees and many very old houses, some of which date back to the 1800s. Ian had purchased a house that was built in the early 1900s. It was very warm, pleasant, and, like my family's previous residence, its outward appearance in no way suggested that it was haunted. But then again, that is true for the vast majority of "spirited" houses. And so it was that Ian, along with his girlfriend Michelle, their four–year-old African parrot, Montique Sebastian III (his friends call him Monty), and their seventeen-year-old cat, Poe (as in Edgar Allen), moved into their new home on what has to be one of the most psychically active streets in the city of Guelph, Ontario (in paranormal terms it is known as a "hot zone"). In my previous book, I had recounted the events that happened to the families of two different houses on a street I had called Highgate in order to protect the residences. The actual name of the street is Merion and my family was one of those covered in Chapter 1 of my first book. I wrote about our neighbours in Chapter 2 in the same book. They lived directly across from our house. At that time, even though we lived across the street from each other and our families were quite friendly, neither family knew what the other was going through. The paranormal was never discussed, probably due to the persistent fear of being thought of as being "crazy," which I have spoken of frequently and not without some exasperation. It would not be for some twenty years later when, by some fluke, I would become re-acquainted with my former neighbours. Not only had our families shared similar experiences, we also shared an actual apparition. Both Tony (one of the brothers from the second residence) and I had seen the figure of a hooded monk. Same apparition, different house. This is a very rare event, even by paranormal standards. Rarer yet is that this hooded monk had made a reappearance in yet another house on Merion Street, this one not far from the location of the first two homes. The home that Ian, Michelle, Monty, and Poe were moving into, some twenty-four years after his first appearance!

————

One Thursday evening, Ian called to give me the news of the impending move.

"So Kim, what do ya think? We're moving into a house near your old haunt and I mean that literally," Ian asked laughingly. I just thought of that old adage about not being able to go home again, but you can always visit and visiting I was. In fact, on May 16, 2005, I had actually returned to 13 Merion Street (the house I mentioned previously) to meet the new owner (the house had *once again* changed hands). Initially, I was to be there earlier in the week but had to cancel twice due to migraines. Our second meeting had been scheduled for Friday the thirteenth, which struck me as salient, but it was not to be. I called the owner of the house at 8:00 a.m. to regretfully cancel our meeting and we rescheduled for the following Monday. Nevertheless, she reported that shortly after the time I was supposed to arrive, the doorbell rang. She proceeded to answer the door and but found no one there. She looked up and down the street but there was no one in sight. Later, when we were finally able to meet, upon arriving home, I found three phone calls from 13 Merion Street. I do not have caller ID on my phone but the main computer I work on does identify the caller and the time they called. It has a built-in, digital answering machine but it is only active when the computer is on. I very rarely leave my computer on for hours on end, least of all to use as an answering machine unless I am expecting an overseas interview. Regardless, the computer recorded three incoming calls from 13 Merion Street. The first was at 9:47 a.m. on Monday, May sixteenth. At the time this call came in, *I was actually meeting with the new owner in her home.* The next call I received from that number was on the seventeenth at 2:01 a.m. The third and final call came at 4:30 a.m. on Friday, May 30, 2005. In all three cases the machine recorded only hang-ups. No voice message was left. However, hang-ups are usually followed by the sound of a busy signal. In this case, there was the sound of static and white noise as though there had been a bad connection. In fact, I feel it was a very good connection, at least for me. Though there were no words uttered, the message was received loud and clear. I have researched many cases involving spirits attempting to communicate through such electronic devices such as computers and telephones. What my computer had recorded was not simply the type of static one normally hears when there is a bad connection. This was more of a white noise and there was what sounded like a very weak voice but I couldn't be sure. I could not discern what the voice, if there was indeed one, was saying. I even employed the computer amplification to separate and clean it up, but was still unable to make out the words. As I said, maybe there wasn't even a voice. It could have been a result of neurological activity from our brains always trying to make sense out of random patterns and filling in illogical gaps.

———

The first few weeks in their new home were uneventful, save for a couple of odd things that they could easily explain away, especially considering that they were in an unfamiliar environment, and with the unpacking still in progress, the house was in a bit of a chaotic state. Nevertheless, they had fallen in love with the house as soon as they had set eyes on it and felt perfectly at home.

Michelle was the first to notice odd little things. It began with the toilet in the main bathroom just down the hall from the master bedroom. She would often hear the toilet flush of its own volition and other times she would hear it running even when it had not been flushed. Every time she went to investigate, the activity would immediately cease. One time when she decided against looking into it, the toilet continued to run for a good forty-five minutes until she couldn't stand it any longer. Upon entering the loo, it stopped running.

She had called Ian into the loo on several occasions to draw his attention to these disturbances but every time he entered the bathroom with her, all would be quiet. He began asking her, only half jokingly, "What is this thing you have about toilets?" She, however, was not amused and found the situation very frustrating, but what could she do about it? The adventures in "bathroom land" were not to end there, though. Upon arriving home from work one evening, Michelle thought she heard the shower running in this same bathroom. She wandered why Ian was showering in that bathroom instead of the one in their bedroom as he usually did.

She knocked on the door, calling out Ian's name but receiving no answer. Upon opening the bathroom door, she found the room dense with steam. She called out Ian's name again, this time pulling the shower curtain back a bit. Ian was not in the shower nor was the water running. Yet the room was thick with steam as though someone had just taken a hot shower. Equally strange is that on one occasion, she heard water running and upon investigation found the tub full of water *even though the plug for the tub was not plugged into the drain!* As soon as Michelle gasped and put her hand in the water to see if something was causing a clog in the drain, the water began to drain from the tub.

Just as she was attempting to figure out the shower incident, she heard the side door open. Ian was just arriving home. Who or what had just taken a shower?

Once again, she called Ian into the loo. As they both entered the room, Michelle stood by the side of the door with hands on hips, smirking smugly. She said, "Toilet fetish, eh? Explain this Herr Professor Freud!" Ian looked around the bathroom mystified. There was certainly no denying that it looked and felt as though someone had just taken a protracted, hot shower. He even considered briefly that Michelle was playing some kind of carefully constructed practical joke but immediately dismissed that notion. She was not one for bathroom humour and besides, how could she have known when he would be home at this specific time to successfully stage this "phantom" shower?

He sheepishly turned to face her and shrugging his shoulders confessed, "Look, I don't know what the hell is going on here. I'm not a plumber and none of this stuff seems like a problem a plumber would deal with anyway."

"Well what are we going to do?" she asked with some trepidation.

"All we can do is wait and see what, if anything, happens next," he replied with a shrug, moving toward her. He put his arms around her and ushered her out of the bathroom. He took another stab at some levity by suggesting that if they did indeed have a ghost, at least it was a clean one and considerate enough to flush the toilet. Once again, Michelle was not amused. As for waiting to see what, if anything, would happen next, *they would not have long to wait.*

One afternoon, Michelle was showering in preparation for a three-to-twelve shift at the hospital. She was in the main bathroom because Ian had worked till the wee hours of the morning and was sleeping in the bedroom. Otherwise, Michelle would have been showering in the loo in the master bedroom. As she was rinsing off, her attention was drawn to movement she saw briefly through the shower curtain. She simply shrugged it off as one of those quirky peripheral vision events. As she finished washing off, she heard what sounded like the door opening (she had closed the bathroom door). She turned, looking in the direction of the door and this time there was no mistaking it. She distinctly saw a shadow pass by the shower curtain. She immediately tore back the curtain but no one was there. However, *the bathroom door was open.* Even though she had just taken a hot shower, the bathroom was freezing. She became covered in horripilation (gooseflesh). She grabbed a towel and was preparing to run to the bedroom but as she was reaching for the towel, she noticed the fogged-up mirror. She thought she saw the visage of a young woman but it quickly vanished. She pulled the towel off the rack and yelled for Ian as she ran from the bathroom.

A few days following the bathroom event, Michelle was cleaning the living room. Her attention was drawn to what sounded like someone struggling with the front door, as though the key or lock were stiff and the person was pushing on the door while manipulating the key. She assumed it was Ian, even though he usually entered through the side door. She immediately went to open the door for him because besides the lock, a chain was also on the door, or so she thought. She found that the chain had been dislodged. She opened the door but no one was there. She stepped out onto the veranda and looked at the driveway for his car but it was not there either. She went back into the house and went to the side-door entrance to check out the garage but found only her car there. When she came back into the house, once again she heard the sound of a key rattling in the door, only this time it was in a determined manner. She stood frozen, staring at the front door until finally, she marched over and pulled it open, only to find Ian standing there looking at her in shock from having the door pulled open like that. His key was still in the lock. She let out a loud sigh of relief while he just stood there staring back at her and asked her what was wrong. She said someone had just tried to get into the house. Ian said that was impossible. He didn't see anyone around the house or street and besides, if someone was trying to break in, the alarm would have gone off. She reminded him that they did not set the alarm during the day when one of them was home, adding that she was sure of what she heard. This would not be the first incident with the doors in the house.

On August 12, 2006, Michelle was in the kitchen preparing dinner; Ian was due home in a few minutes. Sure enough, she heard the front door open and the sound of Ian dropping his briefcase and backpack on the floor. She called, "Hi. I'm just getting dinner ready. Do you want a drink first?"

Ian replied, "Yeah, I could use one. Sorry I'm late but we had some programming problems." She headed from the kitchen toward the living room. The two rooms were separated by a hallway. As she was passing the hallway, she looked toward the front door and there was no Ian, no briefcase, no backpack ... *nothing*. Not for the first time, a chill went through her.

She went to get the cellphone that was on the coffee table in the living room and just as she was about to call Ian, the phone rang. It was Ian telling her that he was going to be about an hour late because they were having some computer problems. She asked, "Programming?"

He replied "Yeah, how did you know?" She said that he had just been home and told her. "Come again?" he queried. She replied with "Never mind" and that she would have a drink ready for him. Ironically, Ian mentioned that would be great *as he would probably need one*. Michelle thought "Where have I heard this before?" She shrugged it off since she was growing accustomed to such events taking place in the house. She made note of it in a diary where she had begun documenting the events that took place. She then resumed the dinner preparation.

[Author's note: In all likelihood, what Michelle had experienced was what is referred to as a phantasm of the living. Ian was tired, frustrated, and anxious to get home so this was a form of involuntary astral projection. (If she had actually interacted or touched him it could possibly be classified as a case of bilocation, wherein one thing or person is occupying two places at the same time — that was yet to come). Quantum physics actually supports or at least allows for such dual placements. It also allows for effects to precede their causes, which is a fascinating supposition to contemplate, both in its causative mechanism and its possible effects and implications.]

The third incident took place July 9, 2006. Michelle was downstairs in the laundry room, which was just off the studio/computer room. She left the door open and proceeded to remove the laundry from the machine and load it into the basket to hang outside. Just as she was leaning over to pick up the basket, she heard the door slam shut. She rushed over to open it but it appeared to be locked or jammed shut. (There was no lock on the door.) She pushed and pushed against it. She began to bang on the door, calling out to Ian, who was upstairs. Upon hearing the commotion coming from downstairs, Ian rushed to the laundry room and opened the door to find a much-shaken Michelle staring at him in disbelief. He asked what had happened as there was nothing blocking the door. She replied, "How should I know? I can't explain half the things that happen around here." After sitting down for a few minutes to compose herself while watching Ian examine the door, she retrieved the laundry basket and hung the clothes outside. Just another day in paradise haunted.

On the evening of December 20, 2005 (their first Christmas in their new home), Ian and Michelle were sitting, quietly enjoying the lights from the tree and listening to Christmas music. Michelle noticed that their vertical blinds, which were open, were slightly swaying. She pointed it out to Ian because there was no heating vent there. Ian said that there must be a draft from the windows or something. After all, it was an old house. It was late and they decided to retire for the evening. Ian went to turn off the lights on the tree and Michelle went to close the blinds. As she approached the window, she saw the clear image of an old woman clad in a long, old-fashioned dress with some sort of a bonnet on her head, like the ones women use to wear to bed. She looked behind her to see if "someone" was there and whispered to Ian to look at the window. He caught a glimpse of it before it vanished. They looked at it and wondered out loud if she was one of the previous residents. They in no way felt anything threatening or menacing from her, so hand in hand, they went off to bed. Good old Merion Street — never a dull moment.

Chasing Shadows

A couple of nights after the shower incident, Michelle and Ian had retired to bed just after 10:00 p.m. They were finally getting everything unpacked and in place, and were both exhausted over the move.

Shortly after 12:00 a.m., Michelle was awakened by a "visitor."

Michelle states, "One of the first things I wanted to get done when we first moved in was to get the fish tank set up in the bedroom. It's a sixty-gallon tank. I was also thinking that even if we were sleeping on a mattress on the floor until we got settled, I wanted the fish tank set up and running in the bedroom. I've always had the fish tank in the bedroom because it is so relaxing to watch and I've had trouble sleeping over the years and the light and tranquility of the tank has been like a natural tranquilizer for me. Anyway, we managed to get the fish tank and the bedroom set up all at once and then went to work on the rest of the house, which, thanks to friends, was coming together really fast. We were so tired this night, both Ian and I collapsed into bed just after 10:00 p.m. We fell to sleep immediately. I had a strange dream … I don't recall it exactly but the house was in chaos. Broken dishes all around, ancient pottery and platters, the whole bit. It had a strange, gothic-like ambience to it. Something very old … ancient. I didn't feel disturbed when I woke up, like you would from a nightmare. Just a bit disorientated. I put it down to the move and adjusting to a new environment. I turned over so I could watch the fish tank to help me fall back to sleep. There was a beautiful, blue hue accenting the air bubbles. It was almost hypnotizing. Then something caught my attention. At first I thought it was one of the bigger fish. He's black with a big mouth and blue spots on his side. He usually hangs around the bottom of the tank, near the sides. His name is Oscar, which, come to think of it, is the name of his species I believe. Anyway, this shadowy figure I took for the fish was not acting like a fish at all. It was moving slowly and deliberately from the left side of the tank towards the right side. I was becoming fascinated by this and propped myself up on my elbow to watch this more closely. This black silhouette seemed to be lingering around the bottom left of the tank but then began to rise up a bit, taking on a more distinct form and continued to makes its way toward the right side of the tank. The figure gradually became even clearer. I didn't know if it was watching the fish, us or if it was a figment of my imagination, maybe a trick of the lights. It remained dark but the outline was definitely that of a head with broad shoulders. It slowly began to rise and move farther to the right, finally emerging from behind the tank. It took a few seconds for my eyes to focus or for me to believe what I was seeing. It glided into the centre of the room and stood still directly in the centre of the room facing the bed. *It was the undeniable form of a hooded person, like a monk, and I felt it was male.* He stood there silently, simply looking at me, or at least I felt it was observing me as I could not actually see a face or eyes. In spite of feeling entranced by this, I instinctively took the camera from the nightstand and just started shooting pictures. With that, the figure vanished and I was snapped out of my reverie. I nudged Ian awake. He lifted himself up grudgingly and asked, 'Now what?' All I could do was point to where the figure had manifested himself. I could barely utter a word. I must say that I was in no way frightened or threatened by this. In fact, I felt I was in the presence of someone or something that was very wise, ancient, and benevolent. He seemed to want to communicate something to me ... I don't know. I had felt like I was in some kind of a trance state and it occurred to me that I had been in some telepathic synch with him but my photographic exploit brought a swift end to that. I had to at least try to capture this on film if I could, if for no other reason than to prove that it was not a trick of the lights or my imagination. Meanwhile, Ian looked in the direction to which I was indicating, and, seeing nothing, promptly fell back down onto his pillow. I did not sleep again that night and in fact remained as vigilant and calm as possible in hopes that he would return. I even spoke to him in my head, apologizing for my reaction and asked him if there was something he wanted to convey to me; something he wanted me to know maybe, but dawn came with no further visits from this benevolent, mysterious figure.

"When Ian and I were having our morning coffee, I told him what had happened. Much to my surprise, he looked wide-eyed and smiled broadly. I asked, 'What the hell are you smiling at?' He laughed and said, 'Kim and Tony [the former neighbour and resident of Merion Street] are going to love this. You just met the infamous Hooded Monk of Merion Street.' I asked him what he was talking about. I knew Kim had written a book about the paranormal (Ian had assisted on it but I had not yet had the chance to read it). He had pointed out the houses that Kim and her neighbour, Tony, had lived in, which were only a few doors down from our house. They had been visited by this very same entity. I was embarrassed that I had not yet read the book, and Ian really didn't talk much about it. Unfortunately, I just don't have much time for reading, though I love to when I can. You can be sure that I immediately got up from the table and retrieved the book, devouring the first two chapters when the monk appeared to Kim and then her neighbour, Tony. In fact, I read these two chapters three times over. I was so amazed I literally got goosebumps. I could hardly wait to talk to Kim again. It wasn't just the appearance of this enigmatic figure that we had in common but our reaction and impressions as well. It was uncanny to say the very least."

———————

Yet mystery and manifestations arise from the same source.
This source is called darkness.
Darkness within darkness.
The gateway to all understanding.
~ Tao Te Ching

Michelle called me that very day. I, too, got goosebumps, which is a rare occurrence for me. The Hooded Monk had made a *third* appearance, or at least three that I was aware of. Perhaps there had been other such appearances on the street that I knew nothing about. The first manifestation happened to me, personally, at 13 Merion Street. The second had been across the street from our house. Now Ian and Michelle had been graced by his presence. Who or what was this entity? Since the writing of my first book, which recounted my meeting the monk, I have endeavoured to ascertain his origin and purpose. Those of us who have encountered him all agreed on his apparent characteristics, which were verified by another psychic consultant for my books, Julian Howard from England. The Hooded Monk is ancient and possessed with an aura of munificence and a deep, almost sacred wisdom and knowledge. The sense that he is "otherworldly" is accurate in that it radiates from a higher plane or dimension of consciousness and energy. No one has ever reported feeling threatened or even frightened, just very startled, which seems to end the encounter with him. However, people have also reported feeling very curious and drawn to him; we were all left with a strange sense of reverence and awe toward him.

Rendition of The Hooded Monk. Seen by at least four people in three different residences of Merion Street.

We all regretted having inadvertently broken the link by our initial reaction. Julian stated that this was consistent with his reading of the entity. He explained that there are beings, some who had at one time been in human embodiment, and others who never took on a physical form, that were conduits of knowledge and wisdom. Their appearances have been documented throughout time in most cultures. Some are recorded as "angels," "beings of light," "interdimensional beings," "the Holy Ghost," "spirit guides," "aliens," and even "gods," which are mostly often found in ancient myths and legends. Conversely, some are also recorded as being evil demons. (Not all interdimensional beings are from higher planes of consciousness with good intentions!) Some are of lower consciousness who take sadistic delight in harming and tormenting individuals. These are truly scary entities that are the stuff horror films and books are made of. Julian went on to explain that some ancient writings represent the higher entities as not only teachers and guides but as sentinels blocking the manifestation and influence of these low-level beings.

This hooded monk unquestionably falls under the category of higher being, guardian angel, or teacher and guide. He is one who seems to have at least one main objective, which is to infuse individuals with knowledge and information not easily accessible to us in our standard, everyday state of consciousness. In fact it has been suggested these entities are the source from which some artists, writers, scientists, etc. receive their inspiration and come by their "genius." Many such individuals have commented that they don't understand where their creations or discoveries emerge from since they feel that what they bring forth is "beyond their individual capacity." It just pops into their heads from somewhere or comes to them in a dream or a vision or an inspiration, which they often do not understand at first. Although the mechanics of creation are not fully understood, it is not inconceivable that unseen influences are at play in many of these cases.

Unfortunately, there is little known about this particular hooded monk due to the limited contact with him. Hitherto, he has been seen by five people that I know of, including myself. The other four individuals possess artistic skills, psychic abilities, and two are trained in the health care and scientific fields. One, that being Ian, has technical training involving electronics and computers, which has enabled him to create schematics that he hopes will be employable in the recording, or as he puts it, "capturing" of the deceased, as well as getting a glimpse of the other side within different formats. Ian says, "If there are other dimensions, and I'm sure there are, there must be some way through technology that can at least give us some solid image of it so that we may gain a better understanding of the meaning and purpose of life and the nature of reality. What psychics can tell us is great but I think we need something more tangible and accessible to the broader population.

Not everyone has a background in theoretical psychics or even a serious interest in psychic phenomena, but a huge part of the population is certainly looking for something beyond 'you're born, then you die.' Humans have always been explorers, reaching further and further beyond our boundaries and boarders. What greater terrain to explore or questions to examine?"

Julian is sure that this hooded monk is one of those higher beings that can give us a glimpse of the reality beyond the one that is familiar to us (beyond our limited senses), as well as helping us to understand some of the seemingly impervious mysteries surrounding life and death. One important point he emphasized was, "This entity is very powerful. His presence fills the room, permeating every atom. What we are actually seeing is *the shadow or projection* of his essential being. He is casting a shadow because his actual presence would be too overwhelming, which would defeat the purpose of his appearing. He is also a *harbinger*. Those he appears to have a destiny to fulfill and likely in need of some guidance and insight. And he can impart wisdom and knowledge as well as offering a view into the 'Heavens' — a greater view of reality. He can also show us the true nature of life and a clear view of reality, which is a mind-altering experience. 'A Rubicon moment,' as Kim has phrased it. These are the people who often change the world or a part of it. Some in big ways like Albert Einstein and others in smaller but still significant ways. Once you have such an experience or encounter, obviously you can never look at the world in the same way again. You also get a look into the eternal abyss, which holds all that has ever happened (remember, in physics, nothing ever goes away, it merely changes form)." He offered a word of caution, though, "Sometimes, *when you look into the abyss, the abyss looks back at you.* There are some who just can't incorporate or assimilate it all and go off the deep end and may develop some psychological problems but that is rare — sometimes in cases where you see something you don't want to see."

We all hope that we will be visited by this being again sometime. If he does not return to us, we will be chasing a shadow for as long as it takes to catch up with him.

In Utter Despair

A few nights after seeing that incredible apparition, Michelle was once again awakened in the dead of the night. As she says, "I had heard some muffled noises coming from the kitchen, which was down the hall and stairs and around the corner from our bedroom. I strained to make the sounds out. It became it bit clearer. It sounded as though someone was weeping out of grief and frustration. The crying was accompanied by what sounded like someone rummaging through drawers and cupboards as if in a frantic, desperate search for something. I shook Ian awake and asked him if he heard this. He listened for a couple of minutes and said he heard it, too. He threw back the blanket and we both headed for the kitchen. When we got to the entrance of the kitchen, it was pitch dark. Ian gingerly reached his arm into the kitchen to turn on the light. Though he wouldn't admit it, he was trembling as he reached into the kitchen to flick the switch on."

At the time of this interview, Ian was the first to admit that he was doing some serious trembling!

Michelle continues, "The light stuttered on and when the flickering stopped, we both took a step back and gasped at what we saw. The kitchen was in complete disarray. Drawers were hanging half out with things pulled out, such as towels and utensils. Some of the cupboard doors were open with some containers and mugs toppled over."

Ian added, "I remember just staring at this bottle of Windex dripping on the floor from the spray nozzle. It's crazy, I just stood there thinking 'We better clean that up straight away or it's going to make a real mess.' Silly that I was focused on this one Windex bottle in the midst of the entire mess. It was such a shock, I couldn't take it all in at once."

We all laughed at this when Michelle continued. "My focus was more on the chairs. I took note that the fridge door was ajar and the title of a book I read once popped into my head called *Hungry Ghosts*, but my attention went immediately back to the chairs around the kitchen table. All three had been shoved around like someone was pushing them out of the way, and one was actually overturned, lying on its side on the floor. We both noticed a strange smell in the room as well, as though the air was overloaded with ozone. We have an air purifier with an ionizer. Sometimes when it's been on high for too long, there is a distinct smell of ozone in the air so we were both quite familiar with this odour. However, we do not have these machines in the kitchen so I don't know where the odour was coming from." Ian added that it was the same odour he detected at other haunted locations where there was a strong ghostly presence.

Michelle said, "We literally held on to each other as we entered the kitchen. We just stood there for I don't know how long (looking over at Ian, shrugging), it must have just been a minute or so, but then we just felt the urge to spring into action. We thought if we could just restore the kitchen to order and keep busy, maybe we could erase this entire episode as though it never happened. I was especially anxious about all of this because, unlike Ian, I felt very depressed in the room at that time. There was heaviness to the atmosphere. I don't understand exactly why I was experiencing these overwhelming emotions. It is a very friendly, homey kitchen. I just sensed that something bad had happened to someone who had lived here in the past. As with the Hooded Monk incident, before we began to clean up the kitchen, I told Ian to hold on and went to retrieve the camera. I was becoming very conscientious about documenting the things that took place in the house."

Ian interjected, "I definitely felt that there had been a presence in that room but I wasn't tuned into it like Michelle was. I don't seem to sense the actual spirit like some others do, which is a good thing because I don't think I could be a technician with these ghost research projects if I became overwhelmed or overly empathetic with the personality of the entity manifesting itself. I think I would lose my objectivity, and as a technician, that would prevent me from doing my job, which in part is objectively recording and documenting the exact events without any biases or prejudices."

Michelle said, "I don't know how you can remain so 'objective.' I was just overwhelmed by the distress and desperation that I felt in the room. I also had the firm impression that it was the spirit of a young woman who did this, probably the same woman I caught a glimpse of in the mirror that one afternoon. *I just knew it in my gut!* There was also intense fear, too.

[Author's note: It was later confirmed by county records that a former resident of the house had died at a young age, suggesting complications during a pregnancy.]

I think I was freaking Ian out a bit because as we were going around straightening up the place, I was sobbing. They were sobs that were coming from deep within my gut. I couldn't control it. Ian asked me what was wrong, assuring me that there was no real damage done to the kitchen. We only had to clean up a bit and put things right again. I told him as best I could that cleaning up the kitchen was in no way going to put things 'right.' It was going to take a lot more than a mop and a roll of paper towels to 'put things right' again. So we went about cleaning up the kitchen and I put on some coffee. Needless to say, neither of us slept for the rest of that night."

Ian said, "I didn't know what to do about Michelle crying. I knew it wasn't really about the mess in the kitchen or even the shock of this event, but I didn't know what to say. I wasn't sure this was the right time to engage her in a conversation about whom or what she was picking up on. I just thought I should let her go through this process, which struck me as being deep grief, and then talk to her about it when she was more calm and less engulfed in it."

Michelle continued, "Later on that morning when the sun was rising, Ian asked me about what was going on with me. I told him that I had a strong sense that this was a young woman, unmarried, with a crisis pregnancy. She was desperately in search of something but I didn't know what. She was also confused because she lived in the house in the 1920s so the kitchen was very unfamiliar to her. I think it was a letter and then some sort of kitchen utensil. I felt like I knew her, though I was unaware of the circumstances she had found herself in…. I wanted to help her so badly. Neither Ian nor I felt frightened or threatened. We didn't run out of the house screaming or anything like that but I did wonder if I would be able to sleep anytime soon. I felt so incredibly drained. I think because we have both experienced paranormal phenomena before, we were not panicked or threatened. We weren't the ones trapped or in trouble, though we were in need of some help! Even though it was only approaching 6:00 a.m., we called Kim and explained to her what had transpired in the night. In spite of the hour, she came over straight away and suggested we call in one of the psychics she worked with in her research and books. We readily agreed to this. Ian, out of a good deal of curiosity, and me, in dire hopes that she could help this poor woman."

I phoned Madeline Kinney, whom I have known for several years and was the primary psychic consultant who had worked with me during the research and investigations on my previous book. She, like Michelle, was also a nurse. She said she would try to set up something as soon as possible. In the meantime, she suggested that Ian and Michelle, who happened to be of Catholic faith, pray for this woman and remember her during the Sunday service when the dead (but not necessarily departed), are remembered. They put this into practice immediately. It could not be known with any certainty if this was of help to the young woman, but it did provide some peace of mind for Ian and Michelle, who felt that they were at least doing "something."

As Michelle states, "We did this every Sunday. I don't know if it had any effect on the spirits in the house but at least Ian and I felt like we were doing something positive. Ironically, the Catholic Church would frown upon our involvement in anything that even suggested the so-called occult, yet they bless houses, investigate bleeding statues and people (stigmata). It also has a long history with supernatural events and still maintains the rites of exorcism."

Being such a longtime friend of Ian's, I was very familiar with his history involving paranormal activity. I was not so familiar with Michelle's, however. She, like Madeline, was a natural empath, easily picking up on people's feelings and circumstances. Both women were acutely aware of things spoken and unspoken with patients both living and dead. For instance, they could both sense when a woman came into Emergency with bruises or worse and said it was due to a fall or something, they instinctively knew it was a case of domestic violence, which, in the majority of cases would later be confirmed. When a person arrived DOA, Madeline especially, would "know" what their last thoughts were. It would often correspond with the cause of death, especially if it was sudden. Both nurses agreed that, "Even though they are physically dead, something lingers in the lifeless eyes and the aura."

On rare occasions, especially with sudden death, the actual spirit of the deceased can be seen by them, lingering near their bodies in utter confusion and shock. Other staff members feel something odd, too, but can't put their fingers on it.

You cannot ignore such commanding impressions.

Michelle treated a patient on one occasion who was considered an "accident" victim. Michelle knew it was in fact a failed suicide attempt. When the doctor on duty signed the patient's release orders, Michelle took it upon herself to have a few brief, private words with the young man. She was very subtle, not ever mentioning the word "suicide" but suggested that sometimes things can really get to a person and you need someone to talk to. She gave him a pamphlet containing numbers of mental health/crisis resources and wished him all the best as she led him out of Emergency. At first, he looked at her suspiciously, but on his way out, he took her hand and tearfully thanked her.

Both Madeline and Michelle, as well as some doctors I have spoken to who have been present while a patient "expired," have felt a strange, almost electrical sensation. They describe a "whooshing" sensation or something like a breeze passing through. On more than one occasion, the lights in the cubicle would flicker when a patient died. This also occurred in the presence of two doctors who just walked away with no comment. On one of these occasions, Michelle's watch stopped at the precise time of the patient's death. She also recalls one time in Christmas of 2001 when the glass on the watch she had pinned on her uniform suddenly cracked. It was 9:09 p.m. A 911 call had been placed by a driver of a car with a cellphone, reporting that he and his family had just been involved in a car crash. The man lost consciousness shortly after placing the call. The ambulance arrived at 9:37 p.m. The family of four had run off a slippery road and crashed into a ditch, flipping over several times. All but one survived the crash, though they were unconscious. The man who placed the call was found to be absent of vital signs at the scene. Since a doctor is required to sign the death certificate, it is not beyond reasonable deduction that the victim who was found DOA on the scene departed at the same time when Michelle's watch cracked at 9:09 p.m. The time of the outgoing call was

9:09 p.m. It was a valiant effort to save his family. When the call arrived, Michelle felt a severe chill pass through her and became nauseous. She excused herself for a few minutes and sat in the loo crying. She said a prayer for the family, composed herself, and finished off the rest of her twelve-hour shift.

Michelle had another experience at the hospital, which will never leave her memory. She was on the 3–11 night shift. The floor she was on included an elderly lady from Italy. Her name was Marie, after her mother's sister who had died when she was only two-and-a-half years old; she was always a loving, happy child. Marie had painstakingly insisted to Michelle that she always felt her aunt was saintly and watching out for her (she had always been told that her aunt Marie was called back to heaven to be an angel). Michelle often took extra time with this patient because her accent was so strong that some staff found it quite difficult to understand what she was saying. As caring as they were, the staff was so busy, they often could not take the time or make the effort to clearly ascertain what she was struggling to communicate. The staff would do what they could and then talk to the family when they came in to visit. Michelle certainly sensed the woman's frustration, as well as her anger and discontent. Marie knew she was dying but wanted to do so in her own home. She had never wanted to pass away in such an impersonal and "antiseptic" place. It had always been a fear of hers. She wanted to pass away peacefully in her own bed surrounded by her loved ones. She did not fear dying at all, though. She was a deeply religious woman with a firm belief in the afterlife. Michelle learned all of this just by taking the time to understand her, even if it meant writing some things out. She would also bring Marie hard candy to suck on since her mouth was often dry from the medications she was on. As the end was nearing, Marie's morphine dosage was increased. Michelle sat by the bed and held the woman's hand until she fell peacefully asleep. Later on that evening as her shift was coming to an end, Michelle began doing the charts. The other duty nurse was inside a cubicle adjacent to the nurse's station, also writing up charts.

It was a very quiet evening but something had caught Michelle's attention, causing her to look up from the chart she was working on

(Marie's chart, in fact). She was astonished to see Marie halfway down the hall from the nurses' station! Marie was heading toward the exit door, which, if opened, would set off the fire alarm.

Maria did not have any IV tubes, heart monitor or oxygen tank hooked up to her. Furthermore, she was not in her hospital gown. This had been a point of contention for Marie as she wanted to have her respectable nightgown and housecoat — not some ill-dignified hospital gown open at the back. For the sake of convenience she complied and wore the hospital gown. She often joked that hospitals gowns were certainly not designed by Armani or any other Italian designer for that matter! She was in a pretty, violet-coloured housecoat with dainty flowers on it. Michelle was trying to call out, but she could barely utter a noise through her agape mouth. Marie looked back at her with the warmest, most loving smile Michelle had ever seen. She felt a wave of warmth and gratitude descend through her. She also had an undeniable sense that this was a final farewell. Marie turned away from Michelle and passed through the exit door … literally. It was not open. An alarm sounded that broke Michelle out of her reverie, but even before looking at the panels, she knew Marie had died. Both nurses rushed to the patient's room. She had flat-lined, dying peacefully in the night. Michelle said that she even looked as though she had a small, peaceful smile on her face. "I know in my gut that it was Marie's spirit I witnessed going down the hall toward her final exit. Even though I was frozen there, stunned, I felt a great sense of relief for Marie, and happiness that we were able to share a final farewell with each other," said Michelle. She adds, "Sometimes, as a nurse, you feel helpless. Especially when the patient is going to die and everyone is so busy. But it really gave me a good feeling that for Marie, and I hope for others, I was able to make her final days less painful and lonely. I owe her, she taught me a lot. I hope her aunt Marie met her on the other side."

Michelle attended both the wake and the funeral, which was gratefully appreciated by the family. "I've never done that before but I felt a special bond with this dear, sweet lady. Like I said, I did learn a lot from her, including what dignity is all about and when it is time to let go gracefully. I was also reminded of the meaning and importance of family, and not just blood relatives! The experience inspired me to begin to do some work with Hospice because we as a society are very emotionally immature about death, in part because we are isolated from it and of course, it remains such a mystery to many of us, so we fear it. We *must* do better by them (the dying). We are all going to be there someday, sooner or later, and I do not think hospitals are the ideal place to meet your end when you are dealing with the final stage of life.

Marie's family remains in touch with Michelle to this day in appreciation for her exceptional care of Marie. May she rest in peace.

———

Madeline arrived within sixty-five minutes of my phone call; a personal record for her, after all, Michelle was a "comrade in arms" so to speak, with both women being nurses. Michelle was a hyperempath (highly intuitive to people's thoughts, feelings, and circumstances, dead or alive), while Madeline was a well-developed psychic.

When Madeline first entered the kitchen, her first words were, and I quote, "WOW! What storm blew through here?" trying to bring a little levity to a rather tense situation. Even with the time that had lapsed between the kitchen being tossed and Madeline's arrival, Madeline could still feel the electrical charge and heaviness in the kitchen.

Michelle told her all that had transpired (having to be interrupted more than once to told to "slow down"; understandably Michelle was a bit edgy). Meanwhile, Ian simply sat slumped in a chair, listening in disbelief as Michelle related the events that had transpired. He looked as though he was trying to take it all in and assimilate it. Being a witness to what had taken place, he could hardly deny the reality of it but he couldn't shake off the sense of disbelief and confusion. Researching such things is quite different from actually experiencing them in your own home. It is no longer objective but subjective. Your perception of events is quite different, analogous to learning that someone you are acquainted with has been diagnosed with an illness as opposed to you or a loved one being diagnosed as seriously ill. Still, both his and Michelle's experience in this field kept them both anchored. Neither of them was frightened nor emotionally impaired by the event, which was a relief to both Madeline and myself. Perhaps the work in research with the accompanying experience is a bit of a buffer against shock and fright.

Madeline had only been partially listening to Michelle because she was preoccupied with the deciphering of all the information she was being bombarded with in this electrically charged room. She finally cut Michelle off (Michelle gladly complied as she was exhausted) and began to convey the information she was sorting out.

Madeline said, "The young woman responsible for this was nineteen years of age. She had the responsibilities of the family matriarch imposed upon her due to an ill mother. The father was mean and demanding but fortunately was not around much as he was a farmer working from dawn to dusk. The young woman had become pregnant by one of the local farmhands. He was not a permanent resident in the area and worked from farm to farm, wherever work was available. Thus, he could be hard to get ahold of. She discovered she was with child after he had already left her father's farm, but she managed to get a note to him through one of the other farmhands who knew the young man and his present location of employment. The young man, or more accurately stated, scoundrel, replied with a terse note denying that he was the father, and even if he were, that was her problem, not his. She was devastated and terrified. As she was reading the note, her father came in so she quickly stuffed it in a drawer and resumed preparing the evening meal with shaking hands. This was disastrous for her. Later, she could not find the note, having forgotten which drawer she had hidden it in while in such frantic haste. If her mother or, God forbid, her father found it, she dared not even consider the consequences. She knew she would have to induce an abortion. She was not sure what type of utensil or instrument to use. She looked through the kitchen drawers for something that might look useful, while maintaining her search for the note. She never did find the note, but, in a hot bath, did successfully induce an abortion. She was later found dead in a tub full of her own blood."

We were all aghast by this tragic tale. Although we were able to trace the family name to the house, including that of the descendant (whose name we discovered was Mary Anne) record-keeping at the time was quite poor, and the cause of her death was only speculation, not an official Cause of Death. The family was Catholic and she now rests in St. Joseph Catholic Cemetery, one of the oldest cemeteries in Guelph, which has been closed to new burials for quite some time now. Upon the uncovering of this information, Ian, Michelle, and I brought flowers to her simple grave marker. This would only be our first trip to St. Joseph's cemetery, but we did not know that at the time.

Madeline was certain that it was Mary Anne who was riffling through the kitchen, looking not only for the note but for a utensil through which she could induce an abortion. She was not only heartbroken by the cad's betrayal and abandonment of her, but was also heartsick and wracked with guilt over what she believed to be the killing of her innocent baby. This guilt ran especially deep through her as she was a practising Catholic and the Church regarded abortion as a sin. Thus, her guilt and remorse was preventing her from moving on or this was not the actual spirit of the young woman but rather the events were being played back like a psychic recording. In cases where an emotionally charged event takes place such as the case here, it leaves a psychic imprint and any number of events, or certain people like Michelle, can act as a catalyst, in effect, flicking the psychic *play* button. Or like radio waves that are invisible, an individual or the electromagnetic atmosphere is conducive to tuning into that specific frequency.

Madeline arranged a sitting whereby she could determine if it was a psychic recording or an actual haunting in which the spiritual essence of this woman was actually present. If it was the actual spirit, she hoped to intervene psychically and perform a type of "psychic rescue" (which would require the approval of the spirit, of course. One cannot rescue someone who does not feel the need for such intervention.).

The sitting was held in the kitchen. Ian had both a video/audio tape running. Madeline managed to make actual contact with the woman, so she was able to confirm that the events that were transpiring were not being generated by the replaying of the tragic event; it was in fact the actual spirit of the young woman. Madeline took in a very deep breath and we could tell she was trying to ground and brace herself. She was overwhelmed by the grief and panic of this poor soul. We all felt a heaviness and despair descend upon the room like a heavy, wet blanket. As well, as soon as contact was established, a kitchen drawer was flung violently open. We all jumped a bit at this but remained seated, not breaking the circle. Madeline immediately assured the spirit that we were concerned, empathic individuals who were there to help. She conveyed the environmental setting as it existed now. A "trapped" spirit is not in real (our) time (though in physics, time is a continuum, but that's another topic). To such a spirit, they are in the time frame that they existed in while alive. Madeline explained who Ian and Michelle were and that her parents were no longer in the house, especially her father, so she had nothing to fear. She did this carefully so as not to shock Mary Anne. Mary Anne seemed to take this in wearily and was understandably confused but desperate. The young woman partially addressed the questions put to her by Madeline (I say partially because contact with the deceased is not a fluid conversation such as occurs between two people conversing). She offered information that we were not aware of. For instance, she did not bleed to death; she lost consciousness as a result of the blood loss and slipped under the water. Thus, the cause of death was actually drowning. Autopsies, when done, were not very thorough or accurate back then, either. If someone had come home earlier, she could have possibly been saved, but that was unlikely. This was due to the lack of knowledge of first aid, the blood loss, and the difficulty in getting medical aid, especially in an emergency situation. Madeline assured Mary Anne that she had been in a desperate situation, not thinking clearly, and that she had responded in the only way she knew how under those crisis circumstances. God was not judging her; she was judging herself very harshly. God is merciful understanding and forgiving. She, too, must be merciful, understanding, and forgiving of herself. It is not up to her or anyone else to judge her. They do not possess the insight of God. As knowledge increases, understanding and opinions evolve. There are very few absolute truisms in this multidimensional universe we inhabit. She must trust in God's infinite wisdom, love, and understanding. Madeline also determined that another thing that was holding her there was her anger and desire for revenge against the man that had done this to her and then abandoned her. These emotions are very negative and of low frequency and could therefore be a major factor in preventing her from moving on to a higher plane or making contact with her spirit guide who could help her move on. (We all have one or more spirit guides, whether we choose to call them guardian angels, divine intervention or whatever we are comfortable with.) Madeline told her that although her anger and desire for revenge or justice was understandable and only human, humans are here to evolve and transcend beyond such primitive, self-injurious inclinations. She must not judge this man and seek to forgive him, as hard as that might be. It is not for her to judge him. She must let go of him and leave it to God. She was only hurting herself, not him. A very tall order, indeed, for any of us! Mary Anne seemed to accept this, however, in part because she accepted her role in the events. At this, we could all feel a strong sense of grief descend upon the room as though some unseen floodgate was opened and tears were pouring through. The atmosphere was still very heavy, but it was accompanied by calmness. Madeline then sought the intervention of her own primary spirit guide to intercede and connect this woman with her own guide. After a few minutes passed by, the atmosphere in the room cleared; a heavy fog had lifted. Everything felt lighter and brighter. In fact, it was as though lights were turned on, although only a single candle was burning. We all felt as if a tremendous pressure had been lifted off of us. It was like all the windows had been opened and we could breathe again. Mary Anne's guide had made contact with her. It was time for Mary Anne to let go and move on. As soon as this environmental transformation had occurred, the kitchen drawer slowly closed. She had given up the search for the letter, given up the ghost, so to speak. Since this spiritual/psychic intervention, no other incidents have reoccurred in relation to Mary Anne. The kitchen has remained intact (at least until Ian attempts to prepare dinner), the sounds of sobbing have ceased, and the bathtub has never been found to be full of water again. No further contact with Mary Anne could be made. Based on all this, we are assuming that she has moved on and is finally at peace. *Or at least we hope that is the case.* As for the man who impregnated and then abandoned Mary Anne, leaving her in such a desperate situation, Madeline had no desire to tune into his frequency, even if it were possible to do so. As Madeline described it, he was a "bad sort," with the vibes to match. Some humans are so low in their development and evolution that they are *dark entities amongst us.* They are living and breathing like us, but they are parasites, lacking in empathy and compassion. In pathological terms they are in fact sociopaths, plowing through life and people, only out for themselves. In extreme cases, they are murders, rapists, and child molesters, amongst other vile things. They never accept responsibility or feel remorse for their actions and always have ready excuses for their behaviour, whether it is their childhood, substance abuse, or even the fault of the victim. If there is such a thing, and one hopes there isn't, these are truly lost souls. We can also hope that the ancient laws and declarations that are present in the majority of world religions and philosophies are true, such as: we reap what we sow, that which we send out comes back to us tenfold, and the law of karma under which justice will ultimately prevail. We usually do not know if such things are true or come about until we are crossing over to the other side. There is one other proclamation that Mary Anne certainly could have benefited from — judge not lest we be judged. We should apply this to ourselves as well as others. People of good conscience often stand in harsh judgment of themselves, which only serves to trap you in the situation. All in all, and as hard as it may be, it's best to leave it to a higher power/consciousness, God or whatever we believe in. To do otherwise only serves to further perpetuate the hurt and pain. No matter what a person's beliefs, it is hard to argue that if everyone lived by the Golden Rule, "Do unto others as you would have them do unto to you," this would be a better, happier, and more peaceful world. In most circumstances, a spiritual release would have taken more than one sitting, but in Mary Anne's case, she was ready to go. She just needed a new perspective, some guidance, and a little shove.

———

They were not out of the proverbial woods yet, though. This was only one of the psychic disturbances occurring in the house. Mary Anne was not responsible for the other anomalous events in the house. Who was taking the invisible showers? Who was the old woman whose image Michelle saw in the window that evening? Who locked Michelle in the laundry room? We were also still on the trail of the mysterious Hooded Monk. Furthermore, there was more activity happening in the house.

The incident with Ian having the door opened for him was to repeat itself again, but this time in an extremely altered fashion. One evening in August of 2006, Michelle was in the kitchen preparing dinner, and she was expecting Ian home any minute. Although she did not hear his car pull up, she did hear the side door open, which was his usual point of entry into the house. She called out hello to him and poked her head around the corner. She was surprised that he had no equipment bags or briefcase with him, as he usually came home heavily loaded. She said, "What, no homework tonight?" He looked up and just smiled, saying nothing. She returned to the kitchen and just as she was wondering what was taking him so long to come into the kitchen, she heard a car pull up. Then the side door opened and in walked Ian! He called out, "Hey, babe. I didn't bring a damn thing home with me," and as he entered the kitchen for "real" this time he continued saying that he had had a frustrating day and the only equipment he was interested in was the television and the DVD. He had even picked up a couple of movies on the way home, which is why he was a few minutes late. Michelle just stood there staring at him. He stared back at her and finally broke the silence by asking her what was wrong. "You look like you've see a ghost." Immediately realizing what he said, he shook his head. Michelle replied that she had just seen a ghost of sorts. Him! Ian was tired and simply joked that at least it was an extremely good-looking ghost. "Ha, ha," was her only reply to his feeble attempt at humour. Unlike the other two incidents with the door and Ian apparently arriving home, this could be classified as a case of actual bilocation. If not bilocation, it could be a case of astral projection wherein one voluntarily or involuntarily projects themselves to a strongly desired location. Ian very much wanted to be home and have the day done with.

[Author's note: This is a very informal and abridged description of astral projection. It should be pointed out, however, that unlike cases of bilocation where the person is actually seen, in astral projection, the person's presence is sensed but they are not generally visible.]

Things That Go Bump, Thump, and Crash ...

As previously stated, the release of Mary Anne was not to be the end of the Merion Street haunts. We were hoping to get to the bottom of some of the other inexplicable events, not only pertaining to the current situation, but possibly the past, as well. Why was Merion Street such a psychic hot zone with a statistically high number of haunted homes, or at least homes that, if not currently experiencing any psychic phenomena, had in the past? (Some of the houses, including #13 seemed to completely settle down with no further reports of any psychic disturbances.) Could we at last ascertain the actual identity of the seemingly endless enigma of the Hooded Monk?

Haunted Halloween?

It was coming upon 9:00 p.m. on All Hallows Eve. Not that Halloween is anything special in regard to seances, but the electromagnetic energy is highly charged, beginning at the end of September and extending into November when it then starts to fall off. A group of us had gathered at Ian and Michelle's for an informal seance. The group consisted of Madeline Kinney (the psychic and leader of the sitting), Chris Howard (psychokinetic telepath), Michelle Douglas (psychologist), and her boyfriend, Michael Duffy, who had lost many loved ones in 2005/06 and was secretly hoping that one of them may communicate through Madeline tonight or that the experience might at least help him to make sense of life and death. Michelle would also be writing down anything that was spelled out, so she was standing at the side of the table. There was also Alex Cooper, who would be monitoring the tape recorders, and of course, Michelle and Ian. I rounded out the group and was feeling particularly energized. My adventures with the paranormal had already got off and running for me three decades before, when my family had lived on this street. I felt a strange sense that I had come home, and for a purpose, not just a visit. I'll say it now and I'll probably say it again: *Sometimes you CAN go home again.*

Most of Madeline's sittings are quite informal so there is a relaxed atmosphere and no heightened expectations. The latter can introduce some psychological elements that can interfere with the atmosphere and possibly produce false positive results. I already had a serious matter on my mind, but we all just chatted about nothing in particular for a while until we all felt a breeze *circling* the table. At first we all looked toward the front door, thinking it had been left ajar when the last trick-or-treater had been attended to, but the breeze was not coming from another room. It was centred in the room around the table. Then the lights in the chandelier directly above us began to grow brighter than anything within their voltage capacity. The planchette on the board began to move, first turning in circles, and then it began spelling out a message at such a speed that Michelle and the rest of us could barely keep up with it. The little wooden indicator was also growing warm to the touch. This was indeed a powerful entity. Had we finally established contact with the Monk of Merion Street? Madeline asked the entity its name. The letters AREEL were spelled out. Madeline and Chris were also receiving psychic impressions from the entity. They both agreed that this was not the spelling of the name but the letters to indicate pronunciation. It was a hooded monk, but we did not believe it was THE Hooded Monk of Merion Street. Having felt his presence before, I certainly did not think it was the same monk but we had no way of knowing for sure yet. Between the psychic link and what was being communicated to us via the Ouija board, we were able to piece together the message. It was:

Let these words be of stern and sound command to thee.
Follow the path of the soul!
Follow the beat of your heart!
Heed yee the inner voice that beckons you onward though you feel spent for there is no turning back.

There is no turning away from the light. To do so would be the greatest of follies and utter ruin will surely follow.
The die has been cast. You have crossed the Rubicon.
But fear not for God is with you. You do not assume this journey alone.

With that, everything came to a sudden halt. The lights returned to their normal luminescence. The breeze ceased, and the intensity in the room, though positive, receded. My heart began to pound when the word Rubicon was spelled out. (I recall thinking, There's that word again!) Yet even though the word Rubicon was written, I did not believe the message was meant for me. I believe it was meant for someone very near and dear to me who was undergoing a major change in her life and she was insecure, frightened, unsure yet happy, and excited. I had this person and her situation on my mind before we began the sitting. I believe the message was directed at her. Madeline and Chris did not agree. They turned out to be correct. A few months later, circumstances would put not only my book but my life in peril. At that point, I re-read the message and it took on new meaning for me. It made eerie sense. I had already missed two, albeit self-imposed, deadlines on the book, but circumstances unfolded in such a way that the question became for me not *when* the book would be finished but *if* it would be finished. To quote from an old Queen song, it appeared that Beelzebub had a devil put aside for me. But this is not an autobiography (and if you are reading this, the devils were defeated), so back to Merion Street we go.

———

Besides bolstering me up, providing some comfort to Michael, and thrilling all those present, the seance did not by any means bring an end to the strange events in the house. (The video recording was not blank, it was pure white. The tape recorder picked up nothing at all. Not even Michelle's spelling out the letters!) The spirit they had in the house seemed to be, as Michelle put it, a "neat freak." There were times when Michelle had an early shift and would rush around to get to work on time, leaving Ian asleep in bed. Ian, who would himself admit, was

50

not much for housework; Michelle did her best to keep a tidy house but she had a hectic schedule so things were hardly perfect (who amongst us can say that about our homes anyway?). On more than one occasion she would arrive home to find the bed made. The first time this happened, she said to Ian, "I'm truly impressed. You made the bed or was your mother by for a visit?" He looked at her in puzzlement, asking what she was talking about. She repeated that the bed was made. He replied, "Well don't look at me," and added with a wry grin that that was women's work. She said she was not kidding. The bed was made. Who did it? Ian said that was an improvement on things being tossed about, referring to the kitchen incident. On another occasion, Ian was working downstairs and heard the quiet hum of the dishwasher running in the kitchen. He thought nothing of it at first, assuming that perhaps Michelle had arrived home early. Realizing that Michelle would not be home early unless something was wrong, and that they had not yet even loaded the machine, he left the studio and went upstairs to investigate. Sure enough, the machine was running and the dishes that had been on the counter and in the sink were no longer there. He stood there for a minute, just looking at the dishwasher, not knowing what to think or do. He shook his head and went back to the studio where he had been mixing a tape. Although he was sure he had turned the tape recorder off, it was running. He swore under his breath and hit the stop button. The tape running on was only a small part of a much stranger event. Upon playback, there was white noise and then the faint voice of a woman with an Italian accent muttering something. He ran the tape through his Mac computer that had a special program that filtered out background noise, and isolated and enhanced the target sound. The only words he could clearly distinguish were that of an Italian woman apparently saying "such a mess." She sounded exasperated and although Ian was a little amazed and confused, he couldn't help but smile at this statement. He also made out what sounded like dishes being moved about, *just as it would sound if the dishwasher were being loaded!* Then the white noise returned before the tape went silent. It must have been at that time that he heard the dishwasher running but had not heard the machine being loaded. What Ian apparently had on his tape was an EVP, i.e., Electronic Voice Phenomena. He had heard of this phenomenon before. In fact, over dinner with friends one evening, upon learning that Ian was involved in investigating the paranormal for a book, one of the guests related a story about a woman who had received a message on her answering machine from her husband saying he would be home late. The machine then announced the time of the call. It was 6:37 p.m. He was already late, as he was usually home by five-thirty. She also found it odd that he added "Goodbye. I love you." In the past when he left messages on the machine, he just said what he had to say, usually ending with a "see you when I get home." He never added "goodbye, I love you." She was puzzled by this and felt uneasy, but went about her business as normal. At around seven-thirty, a knock came on the front door. Her heart sank. With trembling hands, she opened the door to find two uniformed police officers. Her knees grew so weak, one of the officers had to take her gently by the arm to brace her. *She knew why they were there.* They told her what she already knew. Due to the slick road conditions, her husband's car slid off the road, smashing through a guardrail at a turn on the road with such force that he was thrown into the windshield. She was shaking like a leaf when she remembered the message on the machine. She asked them when this happened. They seemed confused and she repeated the question more ardently, asking specifically what time had the accident occurred. They replied that the police and paramedics had arrived at the scene shortly after six-thirty. Just around the time she had received the call from her husband. When Ian related this to Madeline and myself, we could not determine if it was a phone call from the dead or an EVP. It was most certainly a final goodbye; that is what stuck with her. Absent from the message was the customary "see you when I get home." He would not be coming home.

After this event with the woman's voice and the sound of the dishes being loaded, Ian took to leaving the reel-to-reel recorder running when he was not working and he and Michelle were occupied elsewhere. He also kept a voice-activated tape recorder in the bedroom because periodically both he and Michelle had been woken up by the "feel" of a presence in the room, accompanied by the faint sound of whispering. It takes great patience and persistence to capture what may be a genuine recording from a disembodied spirit; sometimes even months. The same can be said for spirit photography. Sometimes it comes down to being at the right place at the right time, combined with the right atmospheric conditions. But persist Ian did. As a professional computer technician/sound engineer and "amateur" investigator of the paranormal, his curiosity had been piqued by not only his own experiences but by the accounts he had received from other people. The advantage to the reel-to-reel is the superb sound quality, especially the clarity. This machine could also be set to record at different speeds. The advantage of the voice-activated recorder is that it will only begin recording when there is a sound to record; that is also a disadvantage as people can talk in their sleep and other noises can activate it as well. A further problem is the frequency level that a disembodied voice is communicating from. Conventional equipment often does not record it even though it is audible to one or more people. Everyday, Ian would dutifully run through the reel-to-reel and the recorder in the bedroom. The latter sure enough picked up either Ian or Michelle uttering a couple of words or Monty (the parrot) squawking loudly. Although they both wondered what was getting the bird so worked up, they were not receiving any "ghostly" voices. The reel-to-reel remained mostly silent save for the sound of the water softener or furnace kicking on or off. But finally, after about two and a half months of this tedious business, on playback, the reel-to-reel had recorded the unmistakable sound of footsteps coming from upstairs. They seemed to be aimless, going from one end of the house to the other. Back and forth, to and fro, with seemingly no destination or purpose. This went on for a good five minutes. It also captured the sound of the doors that led upstairs and the other door that led outside opening and closing. The other door that stood out the most was the one adjunctive to the studio. This door led to the laundry room and was the same one that slammed shut on Michelle one day and that she had great difficulty opening as though it were locked (as stated before, the door has no lock on it). The recorder registered what sounded like a door being flung open so hard that it hit the wall, immediately followed by the sound of the door being slammed shut. Not only was this recorded but it was loud enough to arouse Michelle, Ian, and of course, Monty. Both Ian and Michelle went downstairs, cellphone and bat in hand, fearing a break-in, even though the house alarm had not gone off. Upon investigation, the door was closed and nothing was amiss. The only odd thing was that upon opening the door to the laundry room, they were greeted with a light but very cold rush of air. The three loads of laundry that Michelle had yet to get around to doing were scattered about the room. The room itself, which should have had a slightly lower temperature than the rest of the studio, was freezing cold. Ian went to his equipment kit (what we jokingly referred to as his ghost-busting tool kit) and retrieved his electronic thermometer. The ambient temperature of the house was set at sixty-nine degrees Fahrenheit for sleeping. The temperature in the laundry room read a shocking fifty degrees! There was no window in this room, but there was a mild gust of wind and the anemometer (a tool that is designed to measure wind speed), was used to determine if there was a draft coming from some place they had not noticed before. There was no draft, which came as no surprise to them; they would have noticed it by now. They quickly exited the room to warm up when Michelle looked at Ian and asked what was going on. He matter-of-factly replied that they lived in a haunted house and psychic phenomena, including haunted houses, was nothing new to either of them. As for the tape recorder in the bedroom, both Ian and Michelle continued to hear whispering occasionally, but it was too faint to activate the tape recorder. The one and only thing it did pick up was a single, sorrowful drawn-out sigh. Its tone suggested it was female. Was it the Italian woman? Was this Michelle's "neat freak" that made beds, loaded dishwashers, and wandered aimlessly through the night? Michelle reminded Ian about the image of an elderly woman they has seen in the window one evening. She added that every Italian woman she had ever known (and she grew up in an Italian neighbourhood) kept a strictly clean, orderly house. She added that if they had to have a ghost, at least it was someone who could not only help with the housework, but do a better job than she could. Still, she felt sorry for this woman. Who was she and why was she remaining here? Perhaps she was also responsible for the banging of the doors and throwing things about out of frustration. Michelle said, "Maybe the laundry was scattered about because she was pissed off that we had not finished the laundry yet. As for the other doors, maybe she was just frustrated or trying to find a way out. I don't know. All these maybes! We should arrange another sitting with Kim and Madeline." Ian agreed, if for nothing more than to try to answer some of these questions. All they could do now was speculate. Then, to further support the presence of the Italian woman, Monty was learning new words. Some in English such as "watch out" and "close the door," but other words that they had to carefully write down because they were clearly Italian. Michelle only remembered a few Italian phrases so they would have to have them translated. He would often say *bene notte* (good night) when they were going to bed; *gaurdia adv fuori* (watch out); the one he screeched out was *scappare* (get away) when no one was even in the room, and most significantly, *concluione il porta* (close the door). These are very rough translations and they are not sure they have them correct; after all, they were attempting to translate what a bird was saying! Nevertheless, it was Italian and neither of them spoke the language fluently. Everything they taught Monty to say was in English, along with a couple of German words that Ian taught him. Parrots learn to speak by mimicking what they repeatedly hear, so where was he picking this up from, or rather, who or what? If they had the translations correct, what was the significance of "watch out"? Was it a warning or just something he was hearing that might have been spoken in the past by the woman who may be haunting their house? The "close the door" really caught their attention due to the incidences they had experienced with the doors. He said other things but they couldn't quite make it out, not even with the help of one of their Italian friends, who was only making an estimation of what the bird was saying based on how it sounded. One word that I happened to be familiar with was *silenzioso*, which can be interpreted as silence, quiet, etc., depending on what context or conjecture it is used in. Michelle wondered if he heard the whispering, as well, which perhaps he did. Then again, he learns and mimics that which he repeatedly hears. Something was definitely spooking him at times. Monty is a very gregarious feathered fellow and no one taught him to say anything like "get away." The only exception to this was Ian teaching him to say "call 911" whenever anyone reached into his cage while he was in there instead of on his perch. This is supported by the behaviour of their sixteen-year-old cat, who is very docile and, quite frankly, lazy. To paraphrase Phyllis Diller, his idea of exercise was a good, brisk sleep. Even when it was chow time, he would not dash for his food but rather sauntered his way to his food. However, there were times when he would leap off the couch and shoot up or down the stairs as though he had been cattle-prodded. Monty would become agitated at the same time. Whatever was spooking the bird was also affecting the cat, but, unlike the bird, the cat does not speak (that would be a whole other story indeed!). On a couple of occasions when Michelle was getting dressed, she noticed that even the fish would begin to swim frantically about the tank. Yet, who or whatever was in the house was not a threatening presence. If anything, they often felt they were being watched over.

Frequency

Arrangements were made for Madeline to return to the house on the evening of February 18. In the meantime, Michelle did some research on the previous owners of the house. She couldn't get much information on the original owners, which would have been the family with the aforementioned daughter who had died so tragically. (As I have previously stated, record-keeping was rather poor in those days, which I can certainly attest to.) Being such an old house, it had had many owners, but sure enough, one family that had lived there for over thirty years was indeed Italian. The last name was Fenaro. There was only bits and pieces of information on the purchaser agreement but Michelle assumed there was a matriarch of the family, whether it was the mother or a grandmother.

When Madeline arrived, we all sat in the living room by the fireplace to relax as Ian and Michelle related all that had happened. Madeline's first statement was that since the release of the soul of Mary Anne, who had met such a tragic and unnecessary end, the house was warm, welcoming, and quite homey. Ian and Michelle felt the same way but they were obviously interested in obtaining some answers, if possible, to the other events taking place in the house. Who wouldn't be?

Madeline suggested that because the activity was not localized, they should simply remain in the living room. It would not be necessary to sit in a circle or hold hands. She just asked that the lights be turned down so she could immerse herself in a deep, relaxed state (often referred to as a trance state, though Madeline did not like that term as it almost suggested a loss of sentient consciousness and control). Following several quiet moments and deep, even breathing (actually known as Hatha yoga breathing), Madeline was able to tune in to the frequency of the spirit of the house. This is different from establishing contact, which most often involves two-way communication with the spirit. This spirit was uncommunicative. She was indeed Italian, as was her husband. They had both emigrated from Sicily. She was the matriarch of the family, but was the grandmother, not the wife. She, along with her daughter-in-law, ran the household; however, truth be told, she was the one who really called the shots, so to speak. She and her husband raised six children in the old, large farmhouse. She had one stillborn baby. All her children were born at home. When her youngest son, Alberto, married a young woman also from Italy, they remained in the house with the idea of planning to remain there until they had enough money to purchase their own home. However, during this period, the elderly woman's husband died of a heart attack and the son took over as "the man of the house," and the couple stayed on. (Madeline pointed out that the wake was held in the very room we were sitting in. He, along with his wife, were now buried in St. Joseph's cemetery.) The mother would never have moved, anyway, and Alberto would not even consider leaving his elderly mother alone, especially in a house of this size. It was not long before grandchildren began to arrive. All in all, it was a very happy, well-run household, and as Madeline had said before, it was run by the now-grandmother. She was indeed stern and strict, but also kind and compassionate. She was also a staunch believer in the old adage that "cleanliness was next to godliness." I saw

Michelle smile at this. The woman passed peacefully away in her sleep at the ripe old age of ninety-three. Madeline saw her lying in her bed, holding rosary beads (Michelle gasped at this point but kept quiet). She must have been saying the rosary when she died. Madeline said that the woman was very religious and family orientated. She was protective of her family and home but all were welcome in her home and treated like family. Madeline sensed absolutely no malevolence or any kind of threat from the woman. In fact, she welcomed the presence of Ian and Michelle, though she was not particularly fond of birds (no reflection on Monty personally). She simply didn't like birds because they were noisy and worse, messy). She was happy that there was a loving couple in *her* house and that the home had not been demolished as others in the area had been. Madeline also sensed that not only was she not a threat but was in fact protective of the couple and the house. So as in life, she seemed to be continuing on with her role as matriarch of the household and there were times that she was frustrated, given her restraints. Madeline had no idea why she had not moved on but sensed that she would when she was good and ready to go. That time would eventually arrive, maybe when she felt confident that all was well and good with the household and that her work was finally done. She was already restless, which would explain the pacing sounds. Madeline said one final thing that raised the eyebrows of both Ian and Michelle. Not surprisingly, due to the woman's traditional ways, she did not approve of Ian and Michelle living together without benefit of marriage. They were, after all and at least to her way of thinking, living in sin. With that, Madeline opened her eyes and smiled. She said she actually liked the woman and assured Ian and Michelle that the woman liked them as well, but if they really wanted to make her happy, they might want to consider getting married. We all smiled and had a bit of a chuckle over this. People get married for a variety of reasons but to suit a ghost? That would have to be a first. Ian said that the next thing she'll want is for them to start producing offspring. Madeline laughed and said that that would probably thrill her but may give her cause to stick around for a while longer, ostensibly to help with the baby. Madeline assured them that it would remain a happy household and suggested that Ian pitch in to help Michelle keep the house in order. That may stop some of the slamming of the doors and the laundry being strewn about but she was making no guarantees! (The laundry was her limited way of making a point.) Madeline added that she felt the residual imprint of a very powerful and benevolent entity. It was not localized to this house and was of no threat whatsoever. She received the visual impression of a monk with a hood! (Madeline had no awareness of this visitation.) This came of no surprise to any of us. In fact, we were still hoping "he" would make another appearance. After that first appearance near the fish tank, the only hint of him was the occasional glimpse of the shadow of a hooded figure on the walls, usually during the evening. However, Ian and Michelle only caught glimpses of this hooded shadow because it came and went so fast. This entity remains a fascinating enigma, but chasing shadows is akin to trying to step on your own shadow; an exercise in futility. Until he makes a more substantial appearance, and one which we do not inadvertently break contact with, we have to wait on *"him."* We all have an intense feeling that he is worth waiting for.

I asked Michelle why she gasped when Madeline mentioned the rosary beads. Michelle explained that she had received rosary beads as a confirmation gift from her sponsor, which she kept hanging on a crucifix that was on the bedroom wall by the chest of drawers across from the bed. On several occasions, when she woke up in the morning, she would find the rosary hanging on the bedpost on her side of the bed. She was very curious about this but was not upset in the least. In fact, she felt oddly comforted by it, as though someone was watching over her. I asked her if there was any pattern to it and she replied, "Now that you mention it, it happened during times of trouble. The death of a patient I had grown fond of, such as Marie, or when a couple of deaths had occurred in my family. Other times, it was just when I was feeling burnt out or a bit depressed for no apparent reason." Was it their ghostly matriarch watching over her house and the new couple?

The following Saturday Ian, Michelle, and I once again made yet another trek to St. Joseph's cemetery. It is quite the historic place (now closed) and has undergone some intense restoration as it was neglected and subjected to considerable vandalism over the years. Fortunately, it is not a large place but many of the tombstones are so old, they are difficult to read. Between the three of us, it took over two hours to find the Fenaro family: husband, wife, three children, and even the mention of the stillborn baby (the baby had been born full term; he just never took the breath of life.). Knowing who was still present in their house gave both Ian and Michelle a very strange feeling standing over what should have been the woman's final resting place, physically speaking. I felt strange because once again, I found myself in the same cemetery where I had encountered one of my first ghosts as a child; the burial place of John Earnest Phelan, where years later we would get our first photograph of what had to be a genuine psychic ORB emanating from John's tombstone. I asked if we could visit John's grave before we left. Both Ian and Michelle readily agreed to this. Before we left the cemetery, Michelle took a plastic rosary out of her purse and hung it securely on the Fenaro monument. She crossed herself, then turned, and we headed for John's grave. We spoke for a few minutes about this being such a significant location and about the ORB the now-deceased Paul had photographed, then headed back to Merion Street. The house really did feel warm and inviting. For me, personally, I felt I had come full circle. My entrance and journey to the part of our world and life that remains unseen to so many, began on this street in the 1970s. Now here I was again. A haunted house complete with the Hooded Monk of Merion Street. At the risk of repeating myself, that old motto may not be completely true … Maybe, sometimes, *you can go home again!*

———

Although this is uncustomary, with the permission and full approval of Ian and Michelle and in honour of the memory of Mary Anne, I will end this chapter with a poem written by another young woman who also died both young and tragically. It was written in the 1970s while our family was residing on Merion Street. Its author is my deceased sister, Sharlene Catherine Molto Pollard.

The waves come to greet me with an overwhelming strength
So alive:
Yet in such a hurry to die
Among the rocks on the shore.
They carry in with them
Small little oddities;
A small, red shovel, a bird's feather; signs of life elsewhere.
They seem never ending, as one dies, another is born.
And something stirs within.

chapter 2
The Facts of Life, Death, and All That Other Stuff

In the seventies, I and a small group of friends became like a close-knit family, in part because we had a lot in common and in particular, shared paranormal experiences. We were considered quite strange, maybe even on drugs. We were not on drugs; we just marched to the beat of a different drummer. We were certainly nonconformist. We dressed the way that suited us, not falling in line with the fashion of the day, and our interests were not those shared by your "average" high school teenager. However, living with the paranormal cannot help but change you. Your experience of reality is quite different from those not familiar with it, except perhaps through books. Even our reading habits were influenced by these experiences. We were heavily into psychology, physics, philosophy, and of course, anything and everything on the paranormal. In the case of one of our friends, Chris Howard, they had good reason to suspect there was something "unusual" about him. One day, he couldn't get his locker open and, in frustration, gave it a sharp bang with the heel of his hand and every locker in the hallway swung open! Everyone jumped back, as did Chris, so that the people who were already looking at him would get the appearance that he was as surprised as everyone else, even though he knew he was responsible for the psychic outburst. Other strange things would happen around him as well, but this was nothing new to Chris. As you will read, Chris had telekinesis. And in the case of Marc, he had a brush with death, spending what seemed like forever teetering between this world and the other side whilst in a deep coma. Back then, teenage depression and suicide were never discussed; you were just considered nuts by your "peers," which is a tragic shame. Fortunately, that situation has changed, though there still remains that lingering stigma of having a mental illness.

We were not concerned with fitting in and less concerned with being normal like everyone else. Considering our experiences, we could not have fit in even if we had wanted to. We understood their apprehension of us, as well. We had been influenced by a book by John Wyndham entitled *The Chrysalids*. In large part, it is about a group of people with psychic abilities that had to keep them hidden. They lived in a rigid, conformist society. There is line that stuck with us the most, even to this day. Although I am paraphrasing, essentially these young people were warned that society ridicules, disowns or, more dangerously, fears what it does not understand. What society cannot assimilate, it destroys in one way or another. This is reflected throughout my research in which people would be reluctant to come forth lest they be considered crazy or under some sort of chemical influence. Fortunately, things are not as bad as they use to be, but we still have a long way to go.

Spoon Benders and Paradigm Busters: Chris's Story

"If you believe in psychokinesis, please raise my hand."

Back in the late sixties and early seventies, the world became enthralled with a young man by the name of Uri Geller who could, amongst other things, apparently bend metal objects with the power of his mind. This energy force is referred to as psychokinesis or telekinesis (kinetic energy is producing or causing motion; in this case, psychic motion). Therefore, it is purportedly the ability to influence or control material matter through the forceful will of the mind alone.

Mr. Geller was extensively tested at the highly respected Stanford Research Institute by former astronaut, Edgar Mitchell, who holds a PhD in engineering. Mitchell conducted experiments in ESP while in space and was influential in bringing Uri Geller to the USA. (Dr. Mitchell must be commended for his bold, unconventional research and interests while working for NASA, which, at least on the surface, is a very conservative, "serious science" organization. In fact, they knew nothing of his experiments, but when word got out after the mission, several of his colleagues secretly expressed interest and support. He later went on to found the Institute of Noetic Sciences, which explores consciousness, PSI, and inner space.)

Later, other well-respected physicists tested Uri Geller. It is probable that research being conducted by such scientists and at such a respected institute played a substantial role in Mr. Geller's evolution into a celebrity. Much was written about him as well as extensive television coverage. Interestingly, during some telecasts, Uri Geller's demonstrations of his metal-bending abilities caused some viewers to spontaneously reproduce the phenomenon. Still, the tests at Stanford were rather disappointing. One of the researchers, Harold Puthoff, stated that even though they had the metal set up ready to bend, the sought-after results were never realized, at least at Stanford. What he did succeed in doing was to generate an intense magnetic field and affected the roll of dice, under carefully controlled conditions. He also made numerous, successful telepathic hits. Additionally, he can be credited with bringing the entire subject matter of telekinesis to the public and scientific forum. At times he had been caught "cheating" but he was also determined to be genuine. As for the spontaneous metal bending of some of those watching Uri Geller on television, that was impossible to prove or disprove. There is much to be said and understood about the mind and the power of suggestion.

There was one young person who watched the telecasts with some bemusement, trepidation, and annoyance. I am speaking of Chris Howard, who was just fourteen at the time. He emigrated with his family from Sweden to Canada just four years earlier. He was still trying to adjust to his new home, but telekinesis was not a new experience. He had had such experiences with it for most of his life and was still attempting to understand why it was happening to him and what its purpose was.

From a very young age, Chris had extraordinary experiences. His mother recalls him being able to manipulate even baby toys. At such a tender age, Chris intimidated, and even frightened, his mother. As a consequence, they never bonded. A saving grace for Chris was his grandmother on his mother's side, who was well acquainted with such phenomena. It ran in her family. Her name was Adillia, and from the beginning she assured Chris in no uncertain terms that he was not a "freak," and was in fact more normal than he realized. She also assured him that there was nothing to be afraid of.

When he became older, she became even more assertive in her admonitions, adding that he was normal but unique. She counselled him in plain terms that he had abilities that most people possessed in various forms and to greater or lesser degrees. Some people did not manifest such abilities and if so, it was in such a subtle manner that it was not recognized as anything out of the ordinary or just put down as "one of those quirky things." She also explained that more people than he knew had such experiences but did not discuss them for various and obvious reasons. Chris states that he may not have made it through without her. It was very tough and challenging. He felt feared and ostracized by not only schoolmates, but by his family, save for his grandmother. They would continuously send him off to boarding schools to "be rid of me," as well as employing the services of various psychiatrists and nannies. Ironically, and fortunately, poltergeist activity took place in the presence of a couple of psychiatrists he saw. In one instance, an empty ashtray sitting nearest to the seat Chris was in slowly made its way across the coffee table toward the psychiatrist. Chris remembers this incident humorously because it was so obvious that the ashtray was moving toward the psychiatrist and yet neither of them mentioned it. They would both casually notice its progress and continue on with their conversation about school or family. As Chris put it, "It was like ignoring the elephant in the middle of the room." Finally, it could not be ignored any longer because the ashtray came close to the end of the table where the psychiatrist was seated, did a couple of back flips, and landed right side up, directly in front of the flummoxed doctor. Chris goes on to say that this guy must have been Freudian trained because he did not miss a beat. He observed the phenomenon objectively and calmly, and then asked if this was an example of the things that his parents, fellow classmates, as well as other people, were having difficulty with in regards to him. Chris thought, "Is he joking? I should have gone to a Jungian trained therapist." He simply smiled and asked, "Well, what do you think?"

Chris: It was a fascinating exchange because it happened in front of him, so there was no denying it. He was exploring the possibility that I was trying to get attention. Well, of course, people do things to try to get attention, but positive attention. Not something like telekinesis, though. I asked him to get a grip on the reality of what was happening here. He asked me to explain the significance of the ashtray. When I became impatient and frustrated with him, it flew across the room, again, in front him. I often felt like a coward because things like that (the paranormal) were happening to so many other people besides me, but I saw the circus growing up around Uri Geller and it was scaring me. It was turning into a nasty freak show with a lot of very unpleasant comments directed at Geller. Members of the press and professional skeptics were on the attack. What were they afraid of? Why were they attacking him? What exactly was their agenda? I didn't see them using this as an opportunity to broaden their consciousness and I certainly didn't want to be part of that circus. I did not want to be the ... I don't know ... a psychokinetic freak? I grew up with that. I was also watching the testing they were putting these people through. I could not believe it. I can't turn this thing on and off like it's attached to a light switch. We're not rats in a maze chasing after cheese. Hell, I wasn't after anything at all except to be left alone. I had TV stations calling and newspapers ... I don't even know how they found out about me.

Author: Do you still experience poltergeist activity?

Chris: Yes, but certainly not like when I was younger. I guess it never goes away. I think it just changes form. It's like an inner surge that builds up, like my grandmother told me about. You even get gooseflesh. The worst of the poltergeist activity was always around my birthdays, Christmas, and for some mysterious reason, August seventeenth, every year … never fails.

Author: Any particular reason for the dates that you are aware of?

Chris: I'm not sure, but then again, I really haven't explored it. My grandmother died on August seventeenth and Christmas is stressful because I'm around a lot of family. I focus more on harmonizing and integrating with it so I can get things under control; control alone is not enough. Part of the problem I think is that I have always been very shy and tend to hold things in. I guess you'd say I'm not good at expressing myself through conventional means, so I have to find other ways of channelling that energy. I really should dedicate myself to determining the significance of it, though. I'll get around to it (chuckles). You get tired of it all, though, and I just want to get on with life, such as it is. But, like it or not, this is part of my life. It's part of who and what I am.

Author: A lot of people, both lay persons and scientists alike, find the subject of telekinesis either fascinating or pure fantasy.

Chris: I've met both. I don't know why people have such a problem with it. Hollywood hype doesn't help, either, but the real thing wouldn't make much of a money-making movie. For a couple of decades now, there has been a whole school of thought that our attitudes and thought patterns attract or repel things from us. That we, at least in part, create our own reality. I don't think that is entirely true. There are other factors involved but there is something to that theory. It's the power of the mind, which is comprised of energy. Now, telekinesis is, at least in my mind, just an exaggerated form of that — almost an extension of it. I do know that mind influences matter and events. I don't fully understand the mechanics of it but I have no doubt that it is true. I think it has a lot to do with electromagnetic fields and the internal/external environment. Like I said, it's not something you can turn on and off but I do know you can gain some control over it, influence what direction and form it takes. That must take tremendous training and mental discipline, though, which I have yet to master. There are probably specific parts of the brain involved, too.

Author: In fact, the limbic system, especially the amygdala (an almond-shaped part of the brain in the limbic system associated with such things as rage, aggression, and other emotions), is thought to be associated with poltergeist activity in terms of a psychic temper tantrum or projected repression and the prefrontal cortex (associated with memory, the ability to make decisions and perception amongst some of its many other complicated and interconnected functions) to be most active in psychics including those with psychokinetic abilities. William Roll not only supported this theory but went further, elaborating on the manipulation of electromagnetic fields.

Chris: Yeah, I remember reading some research on that. But there are also strong, electromagnetic fields independently by it as well. We all possess that, but at times it is stronger and more naturally potent in some people than in others. It also tends to run in families, like other things do.

Author: And it certainly appears to run in your family.

Chris: That's for sure, at least in one half of it. I joke that we are the Addams Family part of the tree (referring to an old television program about a "spooky family" who thought they were quite normal and the rest of the world was a bit off). But I am quite comfortable being a member of that side of the family now. You grow into it or you disown it, which can make you really sick. I accept it and am a lot more comfortable with myself now. I think there is so much we don't know about the brain and I think metaphysics (a theory that examines the underlying principles of reality not generally subject to empirical confirmation or analysis) is so complex, it's hard to comprehend them all but they do seem to complement each other. And then, of course, there is the matter of research dollars and priorities.

Author: How was the research for you?

Chris: Horrendous! Like I said, you can't turn it off and on. Naturally, they have you under strict environmental conditions. Even in school, I was never good at doing tests. I'm surprised I did as well as I did. But I felt like a rat in a Faraday cage.* I was overwhelmed with performance anxiety, like if I couldn't perform for them, I would blow it for the reputation of the entire field of psychic research and discredit psychics around the globe. It was a tremendous amount of pressure. I was getting terrible headaches. Couldn't sleep or eat properly. I was becoming very sick and rundown. I even developed an ulcer. That was the end of it for me, personally. I must say that psychic phenomena is not a thing that lends itself well to a laboratory. The individual experiencing it doesn't even have direct control over it. It's not like doing magic tricks. I certainly believe it is worth investigating, though, but due to the

---

* A Faraday conductor or shield can best be understood as a near-perfect hollow conductor. It is not actually a cage but a shielded room. The room shields the interior from external electromagnetic radiation/fields, which we hear so much about in relation to certain paranormal activity and psychics (who generate electromagnetic fields or ghosts who purportedly generate such fields, though I have yet to hear about getting a ghost in a Faraday cage!). The cage blocks external electromagnetic fields, which should prevent any false positive readings while testing the psychic subject/phenomena. Chris Howard and many other psychics have had their abilities tested within the confines of the Faraday cage. Interestingly, there are forms of Faraday shields in the everyday world. For instance, radios and cellphones may have very poor or no reception in elevators. Microwave ovens are another example; otherwise we would have radiation coming out through our microwaves.

unique nature of the phenomena, the research protocol has to be structured to accommodate the phenomena and the persons experiencing it, not visa versa. I know the practical or pragmatic scientists are not comfortable with that and I understand that, but isn't true science about keeping an open mind? I still think field investigations, strictly controlled as much as possible, are the best way to go. Even then, it's difficult and takes a lot of time, patience, and money. For the most part, you have to go to it; you can't bring it to you.

Author: I know you think it is a waste of time to bend spoons and such, but what does it feel like?

Chris: Electrical. Like you have plugged into some kind of cosmic electrical current, at least for me. It's bigger than the individual, that's for sure. It's bigger than the reality you live in, which seems so small afterwards. And my head, from the middle down to my neck, gets this static feeling. Sometimes, my hair goes a bit static. It can be physically painful or uncomfortable but is also exhilarating.

Emotionally it's like drinking fifty cups of coffee in an hour. Yet afterwards, I just crash and can sleep for days. On other occasions, though, that hyperactivity and crash doesn't go away and I can't sleep for three or four days. It's awful. But like I said, it is also exhilarating and I feel a bit euphoric as well. And you feel connected with something we are all a part of but it is certainly bigger than us as individuals. Everything is all about energy. But I am no physicist. I just know what I have experienced and what I have read about physics and it all adds up to me.

Author: What overall effect has all of this had on you?

Chris: Mostly good. I am very empathetic to people. I can be at the bus stop and pick up on a person who is in an emotional crisis and start talking to them. When I'm driving and it's bad weather, I'll pull over and ask someone if they need a lift. I would never have done such a thing before. I feel more connected with people now, which in a way, hurts. I just kind of sense who is safe and who is not.

I still get the odd spoon or key bending. I write down what happened that may have caused it. There always seems to be a psychological stressor behind it. It can be a real pain in the *derrière*. I've read that it may be compared to a psychic temper tantrum. One day, I had a really bad day at school [Chris is pursing a master's degree in social work] and my house key was bent. I was especially pissed off with myself. But for the most part, it's good now.

Author: When people learn that I know you, they always ask me if you still bend spoons, which gives me a chuckle. So, I'll ask you. Do you still bend spoons?

Chris: (Laughing) What would be the purpose? It's a waste of energy and besides, you only have to buy more spoons. When it was really bad years back, I tried using plastic utensils but even they would become warped as though they had been exposed to heat. It wasn't the spoons that upset me. It was things like brass candle holders or part of my bed frame that was brass. There even appeared to be what looked like a handprint where it was bent, but it was hard to tell. That's when I really tried to get to the bottom of things and see if I could redirect this energy to at least stop the destructive things. I even went to a psychic. People assume that because of the PK [psychokinesis], I'm psychic, which I'm not — maybe just more intuitive than the average person. As for bending spoons, which I always refer to as parlour tricks, like I said, what's the purpose? If people want to see it as a demonstration of proof, then they don't really understand it or believe it in the first place. I don't think people are going to believe it because they see it. They will struggle to find other explanations for it. People believe in God and other things without seeing it. As for me, I have nothing to prove. I am done with trying to justify or prove myself. I'm quite comfortable within myself now even though it took many years.

Author: I really appreciate your agreeing to this interview. I know you are very committed to avoiding publicity. Nevertheless, do you think you might ever write a book about your experiences?

Chris: (Big smile) Never say never, but I truly doubt it. Maybe if it would be of any help to people, like raising consciousness or help to generate some research money, but right now I'm quite content to leave the writing to people like you and others, which is why I agreed to do the interview. I only want to help and I think I can do that better as a social worker.

Part Two
Home Is Where the Soul Is: Marc's Journey

I first met Marc Duffy when I entered grade nine. He was a year ahead of me but we hit it off straight away. This was a new school for me and I was feeling a bit intimidated and, like many of the other first-year rookies, lost and confused. As fate would have it, I shared a locker right next to Marc's. Upon seeing that I was having considerable difficulty getting the blasted thing opened, he gave it a sharp, quick thud with the heel of his hand and, voila! It slowly swung open. Marc always did have a way with things. He left with a wink and a twinkle in his eye. I had a feeling that we would be meeting again.

Fortunately, I was correct on that assumption. Marc and I were both artists and lovers of classic literature. We also had the same taste in music. None of the things we had in common were particularly popular at the time amongst the other students. We were thought of as *very strange*. That did not bother either of us in the least.

Unfortunately, Marc and I also shared a mood disorder: depression. The good thing about that was that it served as a firm bond between us. We

Photo courtesy of Deborah Kampf

Knocking on Death's Door.

were more like brother and sister than friends. I had siblings, but Marc was an only child. His mother was a teacher at the high school. They were very close. His parents had been separated since he was eight years of age. He remained with his mother.

Depression continued to plague him until one day, he could stand it no more and took an overdose of drugs. He died but was revived and went into a deep coma. He was not expected to survive, though of course, his mother would not accept that. She was deeply annoyed and even disturbed when her ex-husband tried to persuade her to accept the "inevitable" and that they may have to come to a decision about terminating life support.

She would have none of this. She had had a difficult time conceiving and knew that Marc would be her only child. In fact, she knew seven days after she had been with her husband that she was pregnant and also knew it was a male child. There was a psychic link between them even as she carried him. She would not let him go, especially not in this way. This was only enhanced by her strong sense of his presence; she knew he was not "gone." She came to the hospital every day and read to him. What she did not know was that he was aware of this. He heard every word she read. He was in such a deep coma, this should not have been possible. I asked Marc about this.

Marc: I felt I was in a kind of purgatory, half in this world and half out. I was most certainly not in that body, though on occasion, I could sense physical sensations.

I love the old stuff, like Dickens, Plato, Le Fanu, and the Greek classics. When I came to, I told my mother all of the things she read to me. The last story she read for some reason was *A Christmas Carol*. She cried and choked her way through it. She was in part amazed but not surprised. It was the staff that was freaked out. Mostly the cleaning staff since they were there when she was reading. But I knew other things that happened that really startled the staff.

For instance, an old man, eighty-four years of age in fact, was in the same ward as me. We were in the ICU. When I was still in a coma, this man, his name was Zalam (Sal to his family) came to me. He had the kindest and gentlest loving smile and aura about him. He took my hand. I could actually feel the warmth. He sent to me mentally, "It's too soon for you to go, son. You have so much more to give to the world. Life can be tough. No one knows that more than me, but stick it out if it takes every fibre of your being. *Believe me, it's worth it.*" When he told me he knew how bad life can be, he showed me a tattoo on his arm: A-9842. He had been in Buna and Buchenwald! I think that, along with my mother, was what gave me the inspiration to fight back and come out of the coma. Here was this man comforting and encouraging me after what torture he had endured. I think of his smile often and those soft, loving eyes. During the coma, I asked him what he was doing here. He replied that he had liver cancer and was just doing what he needed to do. I found that last part intriguing. What did he mean? It was his time to go and he was dying, which one is what he was supposed to be doing? He asked me to tell his four daughters and son that it had been a peaceful passing and that he was with God and their mother now. I was confused because he was right there with me, not with God or his wife. After I came out of the coma, I did meet one of his daughters who was devastated by the loss. She was shocked that I knew so much about him, and confirmed that their mother had died and that he had been in the camps. She even confirmed the tattoo number. For Sal, things had never been the same for him since his wife died. They had been "sweethearts" since he was fourteen, but he made the most out of life for his surviving children and out of a sense of obligation because he had been saved for some purpose, which he put down to helping others. I am pleased that the information I gave to the family provided peace and comfort, not distress. They assured me that psychic or, as they called it, a spiritual phenomenon, was common in their family and they were not surprised that he came to me. He was always helping people. Friends, families, strangers … it was all the same to him. I was also happy to be able to tell them that he looked happy and content when I "saw" him, which would have been when he had already crossed over or was close to it. Or perhaps he just came back for some reason; maybe to get a message to his family through me. I will never forget this man. I keep in touch with Zalam's family to honour their father and his kindness. They send me birthday cards to this day.

[Author's note: A psychic phenomenon happens for a reason as demonstrated in Marc's case. There seems to be a connection between it and enlightenment/spiritualism as well as providing comfort and guidance.]

The other "spirit" I encountered was a fifteen-year-old girl named Melissa. She had leukemia. She was in for what had been many treatments. She was exhausted and felt she was only holding on for her family. I told her that maybe the best thing she could do for her family was to get on with living or get on with dying. She said she was so very tired of fighting the cancer and was ready to go, but her family was not ready to let her go.

Her mother was bringing wigs because she had lost her hair through the dreadful chemo treatments. She *hated* the wigs, but her mother would not accept what was happening to her, much as my mother was in denial about me. Both her mother and Melissa knew this was the end. She would not be leaving the hospital alive. Melissa died while I was still in a coma. Once again, the nurses were amazed that I was aware of this information, as well. I think it was the intricate, detailed information that got to them.

Maybe she astral projected before she died or we had some kind of telepathic link. Before her passing, I suggested she refuse to use the wigs as they made her feel so uncomfortable, foolish, and unhappy. It might also give her mother a gentle shove in accepting that this was the end. The wigs were like a form of denial and pretending. This was at about 1:30 a.m. — I could see the large clock above the door.

She took my advice and she and her mother had a good, soulful talk. She didn't last much longer but she passed on peacefully. I was still in a coma when Melissa came to me four days after her crossing over to thank me because it had made things more peaceful and less of a struggle.

Author: What happened to you during the actual crisis/dying experience?

Marc: I went through a type of tunnel, but was *not* heading toward any light that I have heard about. In my case, there was no light at the end of the tunnel, there didn't even appear to be any end to the tunnel. I went through a sort of whirlpool. There were a lot of hands and voices grabbing at me, or rather pulling, like they were trying to hold me back. It was a frightening, smothering feeling. They, whoever *they* were, wouldn't let me go. It was a real nightmare, to put it mildly. But then, from some far-off place, I felt a guiding light, like a strong hand pulling me out of the "quicksand" I was in. There was this incredible feeling of empathy, something I never really felt in life. There was so much being transmitted at once, it is hard to describe and I couldn't make it out. I understand now phrases like "the hand of God" and "spirit guides." They are no longer just an abstract, esoteric concept to me.

Whoever or whatever this entity was, it understood my entire life, passing no judgment but did make it clear that it was not my time to leave. I had to return. I didn't want to (though I didn't want to be stuck where I was, either) but I really had no choice in the matter, which has always perplexed me.

Author: Why is that?

Marc: Well, other people have killed themselves or died suddenly — I am still uncomfortable discussing this because of the suicide component of it. I don't want to put ideas in people's heads if they are having struggling with such inclinations.

Author: If someone has any suicidal ideation, the ideas are already in their heads. Your talking about a personal experience is not going to suggest something to them. In fact, based on what you experienced, it may cause them to have second or even third thoughts about it. You yourself said, we all have a purpose to fulfill. They may consider their purpose.

Marc: Yes, most definitely! We all have a purpose to fulfill in life. Oftentimes, we don't know what it is, especially during those dark nights of the soul. But this experience has taught me that we have to stick it out. And believe me, I know how agonizing life can be. I also came away with a completely nonjudgmental attitude. I was amazed at how often we judge others and ourselves without even realizing it. I have also been left with a sense that we all have a time to go, just like that passage "for everything there is a time and a season." There are people who survive accidents or suicide attempts when they should not have, leaving the medical staff baffled, and others who really should not have died as their injuries were superficial, yet they died. There is a reason for that. It is not by mere accident. Even in my case, I should not have survived. The doctors were amazed, but I can only believe, as I was told, that it was not my time yet.

Author: You spoke of hands grabbing at you. Who do you think they were?

Marc: I'm not sure. Perhaps lost souls stuck in a kind of purgatory. There was this movie that I refused to ever watch, even though friends urged me to see it because some of it sounded similar to what I had experienced. In the movie, this person died but was resuscitated, only she was apparently meant to be dead — I don't believe such a thing could ever happen — you could not be brought back if it truly was your time to go. So these deceased souls were trying to "reclaim" her. Now that has nothing to do with my experience but I had more than one nightmare about those hands grabbing at me and trying to hold me there, so it was not a movie I wanted to see! I prefer to recall that guiding hand of light. I still think of it as the hand of God, if that's not too pretentious. I believe in spirit guides or guardian angels ... whatever you want to call them. They are always around us, especially in times of crisis.

They are there to help and guide us. You just have to be open to them in order to access their guidance and support. I still sense them now at times when I revisit my "dark nights of the soul." I was never inclined toward that type of thinking before this experience. I really didn't even have much faith in my fellow humans. Now I *know* there are spiritual watchers or guides that are available to us and not just at times of crisis. When I say you have to be open to them, they can come in any form, including that of our fellow man. Kind of like that song "I Believe There Are Angels Among Us." Sometimes, I think people have false expectations, so they miss the guidance. They may be expecting a glowing angel with wings and miss the person who comes by at just the right time. Or we ignore that still, small voice inside. A lot of us have done that and most of the time, we really regret it.

Author: That's how you personally access them?

Marc: One of the ways. Oftentimes, I will put forth a question and the answer will come forth in a dream or I will run across an article or book. Other times, I will be busy doing something and the answer will pop into my head. Sometimes, they access you in forms known as divine intervention. Other times, maybe most times, you have to sit back and say "Look it. I'm at the end of my rope here. Please help me." And then wait, hope, and trust. Help can reach you in the most unexpected ways. It's amazing. If hell can materialize out of the blue, so can heaven.

Author: I have always appreciated that adage "Be still and know that I am God," because you have to quiet the troubled mind.

Marc: Oh yes. I totally agree, whatever your concept of God may be.

Author: You and I were both influenced by Viktor E. Frankl's book, *Man's Search for Meaning.* You read the book before your suicide attempt. I mention this because you have an obviously well-read copy of it with you. [His copy was quite worn.]

Marc: Yeah. I was never in such a hell as those people were in, and could not figure out where they got the strength to survive it. He partly explains it when he quotes Nietzsche who said, "He who has a why to live for can bear with almost any how." Frankl elaborates by stating that if a person has "unfinished work he will not be able to throw away his life. *He knows the why for his existence, and will be able to bear almost any 'how.'"*[1] [Marc is referring to surviving the concentration camps.] Frankl is right when he states that no one can take anything from us. We delegate that power to them. That is a hard lesson to learn, though, because life and people can really hurt us and influence us to believe things that are not true. But Frankl states that we can actually uncover the meaning of life through suffering. He had a view on suffering that I have yet to fully comprehend or grasp. He believed we could learn the meaning of life in three different ways. One was by suffering, which I still haven't come to terms with, since the near-death experience, and by doing meaningful deeds, which is a rather Buddhist and practical point of view. [Marc is referring to the Buddhist eightfold path, which includes right livelihood which is written about in the chapter "Crisis Line: Can I Help You?" in this book.] He spoke of doing a deed and experiencing a value from it. And the third one was by *experiencing a value.*[2] Now that one really intrigues me. The closest I've come to that is the near-death and coma experience. We all hold certain values but do we *experience them?* Certainly we do when we pay a price by upholding our values and it costs us something, but he meant more than that. I'm paraphrasing here, but his book took on new meaning for me after the dying experience. I certainly agree with Frankl *that meaningless is a major disease of our time.* That's why I did what I did [the suicide attempt]. But that experience really turned me around. I'm grieved that

I hurt people by my actions, but in the long run, it has turned out positive.

Believe me, there were other ways around the crisis I was going through. I just couldn't see them at the time. I would not recommend what I did even though I gained a lot from the experience. I am just blessed or lucky that it worked out for me, not without a lot of hard work, mind you. Still, I have seen a glimpse of the other side. There is no doubt in my mind that there is an energy within us that goes on when our physical being ceases to be. And that the paranormal activity that takes place in the lives of so many, more than we suspect because it is not discussed, is trying to teach us and show us things. They alter and broaden our perceptions of reality. Our perceptions are so limited and influenced by our preconceptions and prejudices. Like I have said, there is such much more to life than meets the eye. We get caught up in basic survival, suffering or trying to outdo one another. I guess I'm starting to ramble here because I have a class to get to, but these are some of the things that I learned because of my near-death experience (NDE). There is always help there. I know that is hard to believe because, at the time, I didn't believe it. You just can't sense it. But it is there. It's those helpers I was talking about or as I refer to them, the watchers. Like I said before, it comes from the most unexpected places but sometimes, because you're psychically blocked off, you feel alone in the universe. That's horrible, to put it mildly. And don't be afraid to seek out spiritual or professional help, either. That was a mistake I made.

Author: What about your writing and artwork? Has this experience had an impact on it?

Marc: Most definitely. I am still struggling, like I said, but I have a different perspective on things. In fact, I try to keep things in perspective without my moods getting the better of my thinking. Thoughts are energy and they have a real impact on things, especially your body. I only wish I was better at the piano because there is music on the other side of life that can't be easily translated. I can only try to express it through my artwork and writing. But that is not a true representation of it.

Author: In what way?

Marc: It is not truly accurate or representative. If people could feel those vibrations, because it's not really music, although we often speak of music moving us, there would be a lot more peace and especially calmness within ourselves and, consequently, throughout the world. I'm sounding like that pop commercial now … PERFECT HARMONY. People are looking for answers and instead feel preached to or even lied to. I sort of wish everyone could have a near-death experience — not the way I did — because it really opens your eyes. I came back feeling like we really should be in service to humankind. I can't believe the suicide rates. In most cases, I don't believe that suicide is the answer. For some people it is an organized religion, for others it is work. One of the hardest things when you are down and out or lost is finding your way back and reconnecting with life. Purpose is another tough thing but as vital as water or air. I think that is sometimes why paranormal experience happens when they do. It's like a wake-up call and a reminder to us that there is more to life than all the crap we have to endure. In some cases, I believe it's almost divine intervention.

———

Marc is currently working as a graphic artist and, no pun intended, as a ghost writer, and has returned to university to finish his master's degree in English Literature.

He is currently working on a book about his personal experiences while continuing his quest for the meaning of life, death, and all that lies between.

What is to give light must burn.
~ Viktor Frankl

It is with sadness that I must state that Viktor Frankl died at the age of ninety-two in September of 1997. If you have not already read them, I would not only recommend *Man's Search for Meaning*, but also his subsequent books based on a collection of his lectures and seminars, entitled *Man's Search for Ultimate Meaning* and *The Doctor and the Soul: From Psychotherapy to Logotherapy*. I would like to end this portion of the chapter by again quoting Frankl from his autobiographical book *Recollections:* "He who has saved but one soul is regarded as one who has saved the whole world."

That being the case, Dr. Frankl has saved the world many times over.

Marc and I and many of the people interviewed in this book, as well as in my previous book, *True Tales of the Paranormal* can testify to the truth of this statement.

Farewell, Dr. Viktor Frankl. Would that we could all leave such a legacy, but at least we can strive to come close.

———

"A doctor is seated across from a patient who has wings and a halo. The doctor says to the patient, 'After all, you were clinically dead. You have to expect some lingering side-effects.'"

[Author's note: Another after-effect of Marc's near-death experience is spontaneous OBE (Out of Body Experience) and astral projection and what he refers to as a "mild case of telepathy." He believes these are all related to the experiences he had while in the coma.]

Marc: It doesn't happen often and it's not really a big deal. It comes out of the blue, really. Like one time when my mother was at a teacher's conference, I dreamt that she was getting ready for bed and then actually felt myself in the bathroom when she

84

dropped her water glass and cut her hand. I actually felt myself there. Now this was in a hotel in Ottawa, and I was at home in Guelph. She must have sensed something because as she held her bleeding finger under the running water, she looked up and around and said my name out loud. I phoned her the next morning. I was so sure that I had been there that I didn't even ask her *if* she had cut herself — I asked if her finger was all right. She said, "Marc! I knew you were there. It was the strangest sensation." I went on to describe the room in detail and was right on. My mom and I have always had a kind of connection like some parents do with their children, but it has never happened like this before. I could even smell the room and hear the television. On another occasion, I was sound asleep. It had been a busy, tiring day and I just fell into bed exhausted. I do not recall even dreaming, which I normally do. Suddenly, I found myself hovering over the bed, looking down at my sleeping self. I thought, Am I dreaming? and yet I was thinking quite clearly and felt like this was quite interesting. I wondered if I could move about, and as soon as I thought of a place, I was there. First the kitchen, then the family room where I saw my mother curled up on the couch with school papers around her and the television still on. I thought she might have fallen asleep while grading papers. Then I got this weird, electrical sensation and, like a flash, I was pulled back to my bedroom and as soon as I "landed" in my body, I woke up. I was not disoriented at all and felt wide awake. I didn't believe it had been a dream but I got up and went to the family room to check things out and, sure enough, there was my mother curled up on the couch just as I had seen her. I woke her up so she could go to bed and get a proper sleep. These episodes usually only happen when I am excessively tired but not always. It did happen once when I was just dozing on the couch while reading a book. I was out of my body, only this time I was drawn outside and saw my cousin, Michael, driving his way up the road toward our house. I wondered why he was driving Alex's car. Then there was that same electrical sensation and I was pulled back into my body. I sat up and looked around and a few minutes later, the door opened and in walks Michael. I looked out into the driveway and sure enough, he was driving Alex's car. I asked him why he was driving Alex's car and he said he was doing some work on his, car including a tune-up. The telepathy stuff is ultralight. I really consider it to be more of a hyperintuitive thing. I have always been excellent at tuning in to people's moods and thoughts. My mother says that I would often cry and refuse to be held when I was a baby if the person trying to hold me was in a bad mood or whatever. After the near-death experience, I found that I was actually able to pick up on people's thoughts. Such as the time in homeroom when the person sitting next to me was admiring the style of my hair, wondering where I got it done. I turned to them and told them the name of the place. They just stared at me, stunned, and then turned away, saying nothing. Again, this doesn't happen often and I don't know why it happens when it does. Intense thoughts will often come through, probably because they are just that, intense. I also have a special empathy for depressives, but they are hard to read. Depression tends to dampen everything, like a wet blanket, but I can certainly feel what they are feeling. And I knew when a teacher was in a bad mood so I would just lay low. Chris [from the previous section of this chapter] is much more efficacious at this sort of stuff than I am. I think in my case it is a hangover effect from the near-death experience and the coma where I had what may have been lost souls coming at me. Maybe it changed my brain chemistry or turned something on that was always there but latent.

Author: What do you want to do with these abilities, if anything?

Marc: Like Chris, I just want to help and relieve suffering and loneliness of which there is so much. But I also want to use various mediums like art, music, and maybe writing poetry —

not entire books like you do. That seems too daunting a task for little old me [laughs]. I really want to raise and enhance the consciousness and people's view of the world. I was very struck by something the young man who had the near-death experience said in your previous book. "What have you done with your time on earth *and is the world a better place for your having been here?*" Powerful stuff. If I can do that and make the world a better and less painful place for even just a few people, I will cross over in peace. What greater legacy can a person leave behind?

chapter 3
Crisis Hotline:
How Can I Help You?

[Author's note: Although the beginning of this chapter may read as a lesson in Buddhist teachings, it is actually one of the most unique anomalous events I have encountered in my thirtysome years of research and also apparently a case of one of the rarest manifestations of psychic phenomena.]

To Be or Not to Be.

———

When Christian Anderson was attending university in England, he did more than his fair share of volunteer work. Not as much as before he entered university because of the intense scholastic demands, but still, he did more than the average individual manages to do. In part, this was due to his history of doing a lot of volunteer work since he was very young. Mostly, though, it was due to his Buddhist beliefs and the fact that he believed people should live as much as possible in the service of others for the betterment of humankind. He had always been in search for the meaning of life and the purpose of all the intense suffering he was witness to. He lived by some very basic but potent philosophies. One being: *Do no harm.* The other was the Buddhist way of living, known as the Noble Eightfold Path, which is not a dogma, philosophy, or mechanical ritual. It is an art of living that leads to enlightenment and transcendence of the physical and the self, thus also pain and suffering. Attachment (to things and people, including the illusion of self) is believed to be the cause of pain and suffering; not only our own but the pain and suffering we cause others in pursuit of "things" and self (ego) elevation. The Eightfold Path is:

1. Right speech (Do not slander, gossip, etc. Speak the truth and hold your tongue.)
2. Right action (Cause no harm and be of service to others whenever possible.)
3. Right livelihood (Do what you are and you will be happy. Do not engage in work that causes harm to others for financial/ material gain.)
4. Right exertion or right effort
5. Right awareness
6. Right concentration (Goes hand in hand with the above. Do not allow yourself to be distracted by many illusions of everyday life or by the material. Recall the old adages, "don't judge a book by its cover" and "things are rarely what they appear to be on the surface.")

7. Right aspiration (Enlightenment, self-transcendence, and goal/intentions.)
8. Right understanding (Insight into the true nature of "reality." Wisdom.)

Based on philosophical beliefs, Christian felt very drawn to the Crisis Centre. He was eagerly accepted right on his first interview with them. This was not his first time working at a distress centre so he had a lot of experience with the variety of calls such an organization receives. However, nothing could have prepared him for the call he was to receive late in the evening of April 22, 1979.

His shift began at 9:00 p.m. that evening. The phone rang at 9:23 p.m. It was a woman in her twenties, but she sounded so depressed and weary that she could have been 120. Christian answered the phone with the standard salutation, "Crisis line. My name is Christian. How can I help you?" There was no response for several seconds. Christian did not even hear any breathing on the other end of the line and was beginning to wonder if the line was dead. Yet there was a strange, faint buzzing sound so he tried again as though he were calling out to the ether. "Hello, is there anyone there?" This elicited a most enigmatic response. A young-sounding woman replied, "No, not really. I mean, I'm not really sure." Christian replied that that was OK, just to take her time. Nevertheless, Christian was puzzled by this odd reply and also felt a bit of a chill and tension upon establishing contact with her. He wondered if she was in such distress that she had lost touch with reality. He asked her what she meant by that. She replied that she wasn't sure what she meant. She felt blank and lost. She couldn't even feel a connection with herself or her surroundings. That strange, faint buzzing sound remained in the background. Christian thought she may be calling from a phone booth. He asked her, "Where are you calling from? Are you at home?" She said she didn't know where she was. Christian was becoming more concerned by the minute. This woman was in real trouble. His mind was racing while he struggled to remain focused. She was obviously caught in the cold, steely grip of depression and deep despair but he also wandered if she had taken

91

an overdose, thus, under the influence of drugs. That could certainly explain her state of disorientation and disassociation, yet her speech was not slurred nor did she sound as though she was in a drowse. He asked her if she was on any medication or if she had taken anything at all. She replied in the negative. He believed her. His next thought was that she was experiencing a psychotic episode but she was quite coherent. Upon probing further, he confirmed that she was indeed in a state of utter despair and hopelessness. She felt completely lost and alone in the universe. She added that she could not remember a time that she had not been depressed, even as a child. Christian asked if she was close to her family. She said, "No, they are not here with me."

"You mean they live far away from you?"

"No. They are not here."

The conversation was still confusing and baffling. He asked her if she was or had been under any professional care. She said that she used to be but was not anymore, adding that they were not of much help to her anyway. He did not pursue that as it sounded like a dead end and instead decided to venture onto what could be shaky ground. Desperate times called for desperate action. He asked her if she had any spiritual beliefs or belonged to any organized religion.

"At one time," she said, almost sadly, "I did believe in God and went to church but I'm not so sure now. Where is God? I am all alone. When it's all over and you look back on it, you can see how meaningless life really is. I don't believe in heaven like I use to. When you die, it's all just nothingness. Nobody hardly notices that you're gone so what was the point?"

Christian was taken back by such a strong and detailed response. He was not expecting it at all. Yet as she uttered those words in a flat and resigned tone, he decided he opened the door so he might as well walk through it and go for broke. He gently pressed her further, asking her how she could be so certain. Again, her response took him back. She stated as though it were a matter of fact that "Experience had taught her well." He countered that she must have some faith left, if not in a God or afterlife, at least in her fellow humankind or she would not have called. *She claimed that she had NOT called but was responding to his call, that being, "Is there anybody there?" She said it sort of woke her up and she was drawn to his voice coming through the void she was in.* She had been lost and confused and was drawn to his voice. Christian was now thoroughly confused and was seriously reconsidering whether or not she was on drugs or in a psychotic state.

He felt an urgency to this call that he couldn't explain. If she was calling from a phone booth and she didn't have enough change, they may run out of time and be cut off. That might also explain that strange background buzzing sound coming over the line, yet there were no sounds of traffic or anything else there might be when one is calling from a phone booth. Further, she said she was not talking from a phone booth. He asked her what her name was, which she had been reluctant to offer up before, saying *that was irrelevant now* (another strange response). Christian replied that it was certainly not irrelevant to him, so she acquiesced and said her name was Catherine Lester. He asked her to repeat that because the sound of her voice was growing distant; they must have a poor connection. She repeated her name and Christian asked her to tell him some things about herself so he could better understand how she had come to hold such sweeping beliefs. She began to tell him about herself. Although Christian felt empathy and compassion for most of those who called into the crisis line, he felt an unexplained connection and concern for this woman that he could not explain. They were conversing as though they were long-lost cousins. He struggled to maintain his objectivity. She was twenty-eight and had completed university and gotten a job as a counsellor for children, which she thought would be ideal for her. She became witness to so much pain, suffering, neglect, abuse, and the effects of poverty in some of her cases that she became more depressed and felt overwhelmed. She was obviously not cut out to be a counsellor because she could not remain detached and objective. She also thought she had met the ideal mate. He was proud of what she was trying to do for children and shortly after meeting, she left home and they got a place of their own. That didn't work out, either, because he couldn't cope with her "emotional disposition" as he put it, so he was in the process of moving out of their flat.

"As usually happens in life," she said flatly, "once we get what we thought we wanted, it turns out to be nothing like we thought it would be. What's the point in even setting goals? Goals are things we see off in the horizon like a mirage. Once we arrive, we meet up with the reality. Besides, something keeps moving the goalpost on me. That's not fair or right. No more goals for me. It's over."

She was certainly eloquent and coherent. Christian struggled with how he could counter her beliefs based on her life experiences without sounding too abstract or cliché. Christian said that he himself, along with everyone he knows, has struggled with these same issues, including having the goalpost moved on him. However, even if you reach the goalpost, you get a hard hit in the head with the soccer ball (a feeble attempt to add some levity to the situation). She said that the situation she was in now was worse because she was stumbling along through the darkness with no sense of direction and no sense of herself or anyone else. Complete nothingness. "*I should never have left,*" she said sadly. He naturally assumed she was referring to leaving home to live with her boyfriend. He asked if she could not go back home. She replied that she would like to go home but there was no turning back now. He thought she had decided to kill herself and was not going to change her mind. He threw the proverbial "Crisis Line Guidebook" out the window along with professionalism, and became more confrontational, challenging her on a number of the points she had adamantly stated as fact. "Listen," he began, "there is never complete nothingness. Even if it feels like it, nothingness in and of itself is something because it is made up of the same energy that we ourselves are made up of. It is a temporary state — a point of transition. And we are never completely alone. Many people may feel at times that they are alone in the universe … I have myself at times felt the way you are now feeling, but it is an illusion, like a temporary blindness, because of your state of mind. Unfortunately, it is a state of self-imposed exile because we have been so hurt or we are too frightened to reach out to another person. At times like that, maybe the best you can do is reach in instead of out because when you connect with your own true inner self, *you are not alone!* You may be all you've got for a short time but you couldn't connect with a better person than your true self." He didn't hear any breathing and asked, "Do you hear me? Are you getting any of this?" Much to his relief, she replied that she was listening and *felt* she understood. In spite of his concern that he was being too philosophical and esoteric, he soldiered on, even adding some of the Buddhist adages that had gotten him through some dark nights of the soul. Meanwhile, their phone connection was continuing to grow fainter. He asked her that if their line went out (he avoided the word "die" on purpose), would she call him back on another phone? She said she didn't know if she could but would try. He continued, "I know this may sound like philosophical 'maybe' stuff but at least consider it. Consider that suicide is not an end to your problems or your suffering. It is a change in state and places. How do you know you are not taking all your pain and problems with you, only in that new state, you may not have the physical resources to address and resolve them. Most times, it's a matter of looking at things from a different angle, like putting on a new pair of glasses — approaching a problem from a different angle. There are people and places that can help you do that, as well as help you bolster your own inner resources. I know you are feeling like you don't want to live anymore and that it's all pointless, but most of the times in life, we don't get what the point is until the deed is done and we see the consequences of our efforts. I can't tell you what the meaning or purpose of your life is. No one can but you. And that is the sort of information that often reveals itself over time. You have to give yourself the time. Can you at least do that?"

They were losing the connection. Before the phone went dead she said from what sounded like a great distance, *"I'm already dead but thank you."* And with that ominous proclamation, one you often hear from someone who is seriously depressed and suicidal, the line went dead.

For the rest of his shift, Christian could not concentrate very well and was pacing back and forth. He called in a relief worker, saying that he was not feeling well and would need someone to cover for him.

He did not sleep well that night. When he did, he dreamt of her; in fact, although they had never met, he saw her quite clearly. While awake, he tossed and turned, thinking about this woman out "there" somewhere.

The following morning, he went straight to the Crisis Centre office with his logbook and notes. He was anxious to learn whether or not the relief person or anyone else had heard from Catherine or received any reports on a suicide, which they occasionally did. They said they had not, but as the supervisor was looking over Christian's notes, she asked in confusion, "Wait a minute. You spoke to a Catherine Lester at 9:23 p.m. last night?" Christian replied yes and that they had spoken for quite a while, but he was concerned that she was determined to kill herself and he had not "played it by the book."

The supervisor sat up straight in her chair and said, "Let me get this straight. You spoke to a Catherine Lester last night. This same person was a recent university graduate who had been employed at the Children and Resource and Counselling Centre [true name of the agency withheld]?"

Christian, growing concerned and confused said, "Yes! That was her! Why?"

The supervisor put the file aside and looked directly at Christian (as the other two staff members were doing, as well).

"I don't know what to make of this Christian," the supervisor began, "but there is a report in the paper this morning that the body of a twenty-eight-year-old woman was discovered in her London flat by her boyfriend at 10:30 a.m. *yesterday* morning. 'The cause of death was determined to be due to an overdose of antidepressant medication. It was confirmed by the boyfriend that the woman was undergoing treatment for depression. The family was shocked and could not believe their daughter capable of such a thing. Her name was Catherine Lester. Services will be held ...'"

Christian grabbed the paper from her and read for himself in shock and disbelief. He said, "But I talked with her last night! All the similarities? It had to be her!"

No one could deny that the similarities were too much for this to be a coincidence, yet the woman he spoke to that evening was found dead that morning. Two things she said immediately sprang to his mind, "*I'm already dead*" and "*I should never have left.*"

He certainly had not taken the dead part literally and by not leaving, did she regret her suicide?

Everyone in the office was speechless. Either there was another twenty-eight-year-old woman out there suffering from depression, was suicidal, shared the same name, worked at the same place, and had the same boyfriend or Christian had been conversing with a woman who was already dead! As rare as phone calls from the dead are, this would appear to be the undeniable fact in this case.

Christian offered up his remarkable story for this publication in the hopes that upon reading it, anyone who was feeling depressed, suicidal or "stumbling through that dark night of the soul" (it's hard to see in the dark) alone, will think twice and then think again and take a different and careful look at the entire picture, not just pieces of it. He also requested that the chapter be ended with a prayer that the author had been given upon the event of the death of her father, which she shared with Christian. The author shares Christian's wishes and is please to accommodate his request. I regret that the author of the prayer is unknown to either myself or Christian.

Help this special sister to sleep like a child
Through the earthquakes,
Help her waltz through the rugged detours —
even though she must take them in the dark.
May she walk to the lead of your still small voice.
Let her smile at the rising moon.
And may she steer through the night
by those stars you have hung just for her.
~ author unknown

chapter 4
Passages

The following interview was given on November 26, 2003. Some of the names have been changed to protect the identity of those not able to give their permission for such usage. The young man I interviewed is Bill Vandivier. He is originally from New York and is a quiet, soft-spoken, and intelligent man. He currently resides in Guelph, Ontario, Canada and, by profession, performs tributes to the late Elvis Presley — and exceptionally so, I must add. As a side note, on occasion, Mr. Vandivier has taken me to long-forgotten and isolated cemeteries. On one such occasion, much to our amazement, we came across a tombstone that bore his name, but this Bill is very much alive and well!

Mama! Mama!

Bill: My family and I were originally from New York City. My grandfather was a Polish immigrant. He was a devout Catholic. A very good man. My mother never remembered him raising his voice. She just remembers his "stinky" cigars [laughter]. He lived in a brownstone where there were five or six landings in the building.

   One day, he was walking up the stairs and as he reached the top of the landing, there were two dogs. One black, one brown.

They were like pit bulls. This is only how I am recalling the story as they spoke broken English, but the story has been passed down.

Anyway, these dogs were very vicious in nature and were snarling. They had blood-red eyes and began to come for him. He got to the middle of the post and closed his eyes. He had a flask of holy water in his breast pocket. He removed the lid from the holy water, closed his eyes, made the sign of the cross and exclaimed, "Satan be gone!" The dogs vanished.

Author: What year would this have been?

Bill: Roughly, 1946.

Author: This sounds familiar to other accounts of the so-called black dogs from hell or omens of death.

Bill: Yeah, but he was a very religious man. He was the type who would rather shoot his foot off than lie. This experience has been passed down to every generation.

Author: And it never varies?

Bill: Never. I fully trust in the authenticity.

Author: What was your grandfather's name?

Bill: John.

Author: I assume he has since passed on?

Bill: Yes, but before he passed on, he was in his bedroom, literally on his deathbed calling out, "Mama! Mama!" That is what he called his wife. Well, maybe two or three days following his death, my mother, her two sisters, and my grandmother were all in the kitchen. They all heard him cry out, "Mama, mama!" *It was clear as day.* All of them heard the same thing at the same time so it couldn't have been their imagination. They all just looked at each other. It was too much of a coincidence in my mind.

Author: Did they feel anything, like a drop in temperature?

Bill: No. They just heard him calling out clear as a bell.

Author: Why do you think it happened?

Bill: I think it was his way of saying goodbye. It just gives me shivers. Like I said, this story has been told many times and it has never changed by *one* word.

Never Belonging: To One in Paradise

Bill recalls a story in the year of 1979, when a good friend of the family killed himself. This individual lived in northern Ontario and was very isolated and depressed, never a good combination. Being in such a remote location, he would not have had easy access to professional help.

Bill: In 1979 this individual passed on through suicide.

Author: How old was he when he died?

Bill: Thirty-one. He moved up north, hunted in the woods, and fished. I missed him dearly when he moved. He was ten years older than me and was like an older brother. He had his battles with alcohol.

Author: It must have been a crushing blow for you.

Bill: It was. Unbelievable death. I was eighteen. I remember coming home from school to have lunch. Mom was home. She had heard the news about the death and I sensed something was wrong. My older brother had called her with news of the death. He had learnt of it earlier that day. I asked her, "What's wrong?" She was agitated and restless. I picked up on my mother's mood. [At this time Bill was not aware of the death yet.] She replied, "Nothing, nothing."

When I came home from school that day, she told me that we had to go over to my brother's. He broke the news to me in his living room. He said, "Let's go for a ride," because I was an emotional wreck, in tears and all. It was on June the twelfth, 1979, that our friend decided to take his life. That was devastating to me. Like I said, he was like an older brother to me.

A year later, we went to the place where we used to go out ice fishing. We used to ice fish with him. He was a lonely man. I think he and his wife became estranged. Anyway, the following February, my brother and his friend, who was a relative of the deceased, went to go ice fishing in what was this man's favourite spot that we had gone to every year. I had been in that very spot a week or two before and there was no ice. The day my brother and the relative arrived there, it was an extremely cold day. They parked and walked down a trail that would take them down to a tributary creek at Georgian Bay. When they arrived, they could tell by the fresh snow that they were the first and only ones there. This was at about 7:00 a.m. They saw that the ice had all been busted up by a windstorm. There was nothing but jagged pieces of ice, maybe ten or fifteen feet high. It was a forest of jagged pieces of ice. They made their way along the shoreline with a spud [a giant chisel about five feet long]. They thought that maybe they could make it out maybe twenty feet or so. Beyond that, it was all jagged ice.

Wherever they put their spud, it went right through the ice. Obviously, the ice was not frozen solid. It was impossible to walk on. It was so unsafe that *nobody but nobody* would have been able to walk on it. My brother turned to go back and spotted an individual maybe the equivalent of a city block away in this little windbreaker and no hat. At this point in time, it was about thirty below zero! This individual had on only a windbreaker and no hat, either!

He would stop and wave at them and then disappear behind the one of the jagged mountains of ice. Then he would suddenly reappear, either further out or closer in, but never close enough to make out his exact features. This [situation] just wasn't humanly possible.

My brother kept looking at this individual's relative — by this time, they both knew who it was that they were seeing. The relative was white as a sheet. My brother wondered if it was a place of peace and solitude for him? My brother said he could feel his stomach fall to his feet. He asked, "Are you thinking what I'm thinking?" The relative replied, "I don't want to think about it! Let's just go! I get goosebumps just thinking about it.

Author: And this was a favorite fishing place of the man who killed himself?

Bill: Yes. He would spend every morning and evening in the winter there, mostly fishing by himself.

Author: Would you say this was a place of peace and solitude for him?

Bill: Very much so.

Author: Interesting, because those are the places a departed soul is often drawn back to. Either to places where they met a violent end or had unfinished business, or places that offered them some peace and happiness.

Bill: I can tell you, it was a very quiet ride home.

Author: I bet.

Bill: The experience really shook up my brother. He couldn't eat or sleep well for over a month. I tried to get more of the story out of him but it was like pulling teeth. He told it only the one time.

He just put it in the back of his head and never mentioned it again. My brother is the most practical person on earth and would never expect to have such an experience.

Author: So previous to this, he was not open to such things?

Bill: No way. He thinks anything to do with ghosts or things like that are ridiculous. Just a lot of BS.

Author: It becomes hard to deny when it happens to you, though.

Bill: He couldn't deny it and he couldn't face it. Three days later, I was at the exact same spot. We were twenty feet out on the ice, which I thought was a bit crazy, but with those kinds of temperatures and that much snow, we made it out maybe twenty feet and then it just became too unsafe. There was even open water farther out because the winds just break open the ice. I was looking around for signs but didn't see anything.

Author: So there were still no signs or any physical evidence that anyone had been at this spot?

Bill: None.

Author: I know this is just speculation, but as you were so close to him, do you get a sense that your friend appeared at this place, as we talked about before, because it was the one place on earth that offered him some peace that he couldn't find in life?

Bill: I hope so.

Author: You didn't indicate that he was waving as though in distress. You seemed to be suggesting that it was more like he was waving hello or goodbye. Is that accurate?

Bill: I'm not sure. I just know that no human on this earth could do what he was doing. Out there in those frigid temperatures, walking on shards of ice and in nothing but a windbreaker and no hat!

Author: Did he leave a note or anything that indicated his intentions to kill himself?

Bill: He did leave a note but I don't know what was said in it.

Author: Sometimes the pain is just so overwhelming. It seems to swallow you whole. That, combined with the isolation and drinking … we can't be judges.

Bill: That's right. It was a real shocker, though. We went back the following spring. We were waiting in the car for the sun to rise so we could go fishing. I asked my brother about the experience again, but he said that he didn't want to think about it. The

Photo courtesy of William Vandivier

Fishing spot where the spirit of the suicide victim was seen by two witnesses on the ice-covered water with shards of ice jutting up.

experience greatly bothered him. I've been back many times but have never seen anything.

Author: Perhaps he has moved on and is finally at peace.

Bill: Right. He died in June. I'm sure he has moved on now.

Teddy's Footsteps

Author: You mentioned an incident that took place after your father died.

Bill: Yes. This would have been in 1983. My mom and I were watching television when I distinctly heard footsteps coming from upstairs. I asked my mom to turn the television down and then she heard them, too. I was really fearful that a burglar or someone had broken into the house. I went upstairs to investigate, but found nothing. The next day, it occurred to me that it was my father, even though he rarely went upstairs.

Another strange incident happened when my mom was in the hospital. She had a dog for seventeen years, a corgi. His name was Teddy. He was very depressed by her absence. He would just mope around and go in and out of her room.

Finally, he became very ill and I had to have him put down. It was one of the hardest things I ever had to do. I didn't want to tell Mom about having to put him down, but when I went to see her in the hospital on a second visit, I was about to tell her when she said, "You had to put Teddy down. I know."

Not long after I put the dog down, out of the corner of my eye, I saw the back half of Teddy turning the corner. Strangely, though, he was radiating a light, like an aura. I later found out that my wife, Cathy, had the same experience. She also witnessed the back half of the dog, glowing while turning the corner. I said to her, "You won't believe what I just saw. And she said you won't believe what I saw!" We had both seen the same thing. We are very practical people, not prone to this sort of stuff.

Author: I hear that quite often. "We're not the type of people this sort of thing happens to." It is a very common refrain, but paranormal experiences cross all cultures, backgrounds, and age ... just about everything. It does not discriminate. Ironically, I have spoken to people who wish very much to have such an experience and nothing ever happens to them. One of those unsolved mysteries. Why to some and not others? Is it internal or external or a combination of factors? A combination of electromagnetic fields that converge with other internal and external factors. Many people with psychic tendencies have stated that sometimes they are hyperaware and ultrasensitive. Other times, it is as though a switch has been turned off in them. The weather, with the negatively charged ions, can trigger events, as well. This could also be an explanation for why spirits or paranormal activity occurs at certain times and not others.

Bill had another experience that he will never forget.

He had a childhood friend who lost his mother two days before Bill came to visit him. It was ten o'clock in the morning and he had no sooner stepped through the door when the phone rang. His bereaved friend was upstairs, so Bill answered the phoned. He was greeted with a bizarre-sounding type of static. He described it as a "bzzzzzzzz" kind of noise. It was not the normal type of static sound you would encounter with regular phone difficulties. This same event was to repeat itself later that same night at ten o'clock. Bill suggested to his friend that it was his mother calling to let him know she was all right, and he was not alone. Whether it was a call from the other side or not (as we have no way of knowing), it was very comforting to Bill's friend.

In my previous book, I wrote about a phone call a woman received from her deceased husband, only in this case, she clearly heard his voice. At the time, there was a storm coming so the atmosphere would have been saturated with negatively charged ions, which is a highly conducive atmosphere for a variety of paranormal activity, including those involving electricity-operated apparatuses such as televisions, computers, and telephones. Still, this is only one of many theories (you will read more about this form of manifestation throughout this book).

Calling Out the Dead

Many years ago, Bill was driving home from a night out with his friends. They were coming up to a place known as "ghost road," so named because although there is no graveyard nearby, there is a tombstone on a slight hill. The stone commemorates the final resting place of both a father and his son. It was an unusual place for a tombstone as there are no cemeteries nearby and it is in an isolated location.

Bill decided that he was going to get out of the car and sit by the tombstone, to see if he could pick something up or perhaps it was simply youthful naivete and curiosity. A friend of his in the car warned him not to mess with this. It was, at the very least, disrespectful. Nevertheless,

Picture of Bill Vandivier at enigmatic Memorial stone on "Ghost Hill."

Bill asked to be dropped off and that they were to drive down the road and return to pick him up in ten minutes. Much to his friends' chagrin, they agreed to do this.

They dropped Bill off and he sat quietly in the dark by the monument. He began to feel a little nervous to say the least. He suddenly began to hear a noise coming up from behind him. It was the sound of twigs being snapped, as though someone or something was coming toward where he was sitting. It was much too loud and pronounced to be an animal. It was then that he became truly frightened and quite anxious for his friends to return. Meanwhile, during his wait, the sounds were coming closer and closer. Finally, he saw the headlights of the car returning for him. He was never so relieved in his life!

It was not just the sound, but a gut feeling that he had no business being there, and was definitely not welcome.

Bill was by trade a professional restorer of antique furniture. He was quite good at his job. However, the day following his visit to the gravesite, he dropped no less than two panes of glass, as though they had just been whipped out of his hands. Nothing like this had ever happened to him before. There were also other problems with machinery that had just been serviced. Was it all just a coincidence or maybe he was still shaken up by the previous night's adventure? Or maybe it was something more otherworldly that had resented his presence at the monument. Whatever the cause, it was lucky that he was not injured on the job site.

Bill took me out to see this site recently. After photographing Bill at the site, the flash on my camera would not turn off; in fact, it was flashing like crazy. The following day, my answering machine malfunctioned. It was recording what sounded like radio stations, and the final message ended with what sounded like a tire squealing.

Bill won't be returning to that site any time soon; only on my account as I am investigating it to determine, amongst other things, why this monument is in such a strange location and why the father and son are in the same plot. That in and of itself is not unusual since families are often buried in the same plot, but why just the father and son and why at this rather odd location? There is probably a logical explanation but at this point, that has not been determined. It could simply be that there was a stipulation in the will and the family may have had a long, familiar attachment to the land, but how they died and the location of the rest of the family is unknown. We did run into an individual walking his dog who had lived there for quite some time and said that a long time ago, there was a graveyard there but all that remained was this single monument. Why? He did not know where the other remains had been moved to. For now, it remains a mystery … but only for now. In the meantime, may they both rest in peace.

chapter 5
Things That Go Bump
in the Night (and the Day)

[Author's note: Dedications are usually reserved for the beginning of a book but given the contents of this portion of the book, I feel compelled to dedicate this to the two men who died in the private plane crash and to the one hundred and one people who died in the crash of flight 401.]

Photo courtesy of Deborah Kampf

"Six Feet Under" diner.

———

In my previous book, I had written about a phenomenon clinically known as sleep paralysis. In mythos, it is referred to as the old hag syndrome. Reports of such experiences date back to ancient times and have been given many names, including "the succubus" in which a vampire-like creature would position itself on the chest of an individual and suck the life out of them (babies would often be the victims but their deaths were more likely a result of SIDS [Sudden Infant Death Syndrome], which they knew nothing about in those days). There are clinical explanations for these forms of "dream experiences" and they are fairly common throughout the population. They most often occur during the deepest stage of sleep known as NREM (Non-Rapid Eye Movement) but also commonly occur when one is waking up in the morning while in a hypnopompic state or falling to sleep (hypnagogic state). These are natural altered states of consciousness very rarely associated with any medical illness.

One of the people whose story was featured in my previous book (known as Katrina) shares such a dream experience with a supernatural twist.

Katrina: Although I was staying at my grandparents' farm at the time, the dream did not actually take place there.

In the dream, I saw a plane crash right in front of the farmhouse. [The family farm had a private "airport."] I was standing outside when it happened. Curiously, the plane didn't blow up, as it would have in real life. However, it was smoking and a complete wreck. The tail was standing up but the cockpit was completely demolished. I knew that whoever was in that plane would be dead. Because it was my grandfather's plane, I assumed it was he who was the victim. I remember walking around the crash site in absolute horror. I recall *every detail of it*. It felt *so* real! As I walked around the site, I felt utterly helpless and in absolute horror. Usually, when I have a horrific nightmare, they wake me up but this time I remained asleep, just observing the crash site.

Author: Did you feel as though you were there?

Katrina: Exactly. I didn't know what to do. I knew I couldn't get the pilot out of the plane because the front of the plane was crushed beyond all hope. Then, many years later, my uncle was flying my grandfather's plane with another chap. [This was not a dream. It really happened.] Shortly after takeoff, the plane banked [veered sharply] left toward a row of houses that were in the path of the plane. Witnesses thought he was having trouble getting back to the runway. It made another sharp bank to avoid the houses. [Author's note: Although it can never be known, it can be a reasonable estimation given the nature of her uncle that he knew they were going to crash and changed directions to avoid the houses. A very noble deed.] At that point it just nose-dived into the ground and burst into flames. My uncle was killed instantly. Neighbours tried to pull the other chap out of the burning plane but he later died in a hospital in Hamilton, Ontario. The similarities were that it was my grandfather's plane and that it took off from the same runway and nose-dived into the ground. The occupants were killed. Because of all the similarities between this real event and my dream, I just knew the dream had to have been a premonition.

Author: For the readers who have not read about you in my first book, your grandmother saw the spirit of the uncle who was killed in that crash?

Katrina: Yes. He was always very close to my grandmother. Grandma lived in a condominium and asked him if he could come over some time and give her a price for painting the walls. He was a painter by trade. Shortly after the crash, of which she knew nothing of at the time, she was sitting quietly in her chair sewing on some buttons when out of the corner of her eye, she caught a glimpse of movement. She turned to see what it was and saw a man in her kitchen. He appeared as a solid form, not vaporous or anything like that. She believed it was a real man. He was walking through her kitchen — you can see the kitchen from the living room because the two rooms are only divided by a circular island/bar. As she had a view to the only entrance into the condominium, she could not understand how anyone had gotten in without her seeing.

She was frozen in fear. This "person" never looked at her directly, as though she were not even there. He left the kitchen and entered the dining room area. His head was turned in the opposite direction of her and he seemed to be examining the wall just as one would do if he were sizing up an estimate for a paint job!

She could make out many details about him. For instance, she could make out his size and build. He had a broad back. She could ascertain the colour of his hair and even that it curled up at the back of his neck, just as my uncle had looked in life when he was alive.

She went on to describe the clothes he had on. He was wearing an old T-shirt that was faded the way clothes do when they are washed very often. About an hour after the crash, I called her trying to track down my mom to tell her about the plane crash. I was in a bit of a panic myself and wanted to get off the phone quickly. At the time, I could not understand why Grandma was apparently trying to keep me on the phone. I had no way of knowing what a fearful experience she was having. She was just so relieved to hear the voice of a living human being. Later, when she shared her experience with me, it became obvious why she was so desperate to keep me on the phone. We also learned that at the time of his death my uncle was wearing the T-shirt that my Grandma had seen the ghostly visitor in. His widow later confirmed that it was his favourite shirt, so much so that it would no sooner come out of the dryer after having been washed, and as it was so many times, it was indeed faded, that he would put it right on. Like I said in our first interview, Grandma told me that before this experience, she was never sure about such things as ghosts, but if someone were to ask her now, her reply would be that she does not simply believe they exist, *she knows they do!*

Photo courtesy of Deborah Kampf

"Final Destination." Picture of hangar from which the private plane emerged from on its fatal flight.

The tragic event of this plane crash brings to mind the events surrounding another horrific crash that was also followed by a haunting, albeit of somewhat greater magnitude and broader consequence. I first heard the story of this crash and the events that followed it when I was in my early teens. It had a tremendous impact on me and, if you will pardon the pun, has left me haunted till this day.

On December 29, 1972, flight 401 of Eastern Airlines L-1011, TriStar jumbo jet, crashed into a Florida swamp. The crash was of such intensity that passengers were found still strapped in their seats but their clothing and the upholstery of the seats were stripped off. I still have visions of those poor, helpless victims, at least the few who survived (a mere seventy people escaped with their lives while 101 were killed), being trapped in their seats in the cold murky waters of the deep, dark swamp wondering and shuddering at every sound of something splashing into the water, echoing through the black night in the swamp. Amongst the dead were Captain Robert Loft, who was trapped in the cockpit and Second Officer Don Repo, who had been rescued but later died in the hospital. It was Don Repo who noticed that the plane was flying far too close and fast to the ground even though the flight control panels indicated that the plane was actually flying at a much higher altitude. By the time the pilot and second officer realized that the panels were faulty, it was too late and the plane made its fatal plunge into its watery grave.

In spite of the nightmarish crash, its cause was determined to be a result of minor faults in the control panel, so parts of the plane were salvaged and installed in other planes. Not much longer after the crash, the ghosts of Captain Robert Loft and Second Officer Don Repo were seen on the planes that contained the salvaged parts of the doomed airliner. They were seen by well over twenty people including flight attendants, passengers, and pilots. One witness, perhaps ironically, was none other than one of the vice presidents of Eastern Airlines. While chatting away with a fully uniformed pilot sitting near him, it suddenly dawned on him that this pilot looked just like Captain Loft. Upon that realization, the captain simply vanished! Similar encounters with the captain have happened to others flying on planes with the salvaged parts. In another incident, it was Don Repo who had been seen by a passenger. She became concerned when a man nearby her looked as though he was becoming deathly ill. She called a flight attendant for assistance, upon which time the man doubled over and vanished in front of several witnesses. On another occasion, the flight attendants were in the galley preparing the meals. As if airline food were not scary enough, when one of the flight attendants by the name of Faye Merryweather was closing the small oven doors, she clearly saw the visage of Don Repo in the glass door of one of the ovens. She was terribly shaken up and backed out of the galley right into one of the other attendants. She tearfully related to her co-worker what she had just witnessed. There was no mistaking the face she had seen because she had been on many flights with Don Repo before. In yet another visit by made by Repo, a flight engineer was running through the pre-flight inspection when Repo appeared to him and clearly stated, "You don't need to worry about the pre-flight, I've already done it." On another occasion, three witnesses, including a flight engineer who had known him quite well, all saw Don Repo and heard him state quite clearly, "Watch out for fire on this plane." At the time, there was certainly no fire anywhere on the aircraft, but not long after take off, an engine did indeed catch fire and the plane made an emergency landing. This was not to be the only warning staff would receive regarding a flight.

On the next occasion it was Captain Loft who was seen by the captain and three crew members before a flight set to depart from JFK International Airport. The encounter so unsettled them that they cancelled the flight. What might have unfolded will never be known because of the cancellation. However, the rescheduled flight was uneventful. A standby pilot was called in as it was assumed that the scheduled pilot had "taken ill." Perhaps it was just a matter of timing, as it only takes a second to change a life or many lives forever. One imposing appearance due to the nature of the message was that of Repo, who, when he appeared to the captain said with conviction, "There will never be another crash. We will not allow it." There had been many other recorded incidents involving the not-so-departed spirits of Don Repo and Robert Loft, in fact too many by so-called "reputable" witnesses that Eastern Airlines could not suppress or manage the stories that by now, were in wide circulation. Reports of all the incidents were reported to the Flight Safety Foundation who commented that the reports "were given by experienced and trustworthy pilots and crew. We consider them significant." All this was unprecedented in terms of paranormal activity, but psychical research was prevented by Eastern Airlines, who considered the entire affair bad for business. Eastern Airlines quietly had the salvaged parts from the doomed airliner removed from all the planes the parts had been installed in. However, this action did not stop the stories from circulating (in fact a book and a movie resulted from this extraordinary haunting and, as is evident by the retelling of the events here, it is still being talked about); it did apparently bring an end to any more sightings of these two determined souls. *If, in fact it was a result of removing the salvaged remains of flight 401.* It may have been a result of something else altogether: it has been reported that a small group of Eastern Airlines staff (some of which were confused and skeptical), with the help of a medium, held an informal seance of a sort. It was more of a spiritual intervention to help the souls move on as the medium indicated that the two men felt overwhelming guilt and responsibility for the crash and subsequent loss of lives. This is a plausible supposition since during one encounter between another pilot and Don Repo, the latter reportedly made it clear that *"There will never be another crash. We will not let it happen."* If there is validity to the theory that some hauntings are caused by a sudden and tragic death, this would certainly qualify as these two men were alive during and after the crash. They saw what was coming and what they were headed for, the swamp, but despite their desperation, were helpless to do anything about it. The crash took place within a matter of seconds. However, as previously stated, Captain Loft was trapped in the cockpit for at least *an hour* before he died. Guilt is another emotion that can trap a spirit while they attempt to make things right. In this case, it was unnecessary guilt as no one was at fault.

The informal group included two pilots. All in the group were quite careful in keeping their involvement with this event secret for fear of their reputations or even their position within the company. After establishing contact with the two souls, the medium assured them that they had done everything they could. It was a mechanical failure; the fault did not lay with them. It was now time for them to let go of the event and move on. All those in the room claim to have not only felt the presence of the two spirits but their peaceful departure, as well. Whether it was the removal of the salvaged parts or the spiritual intervention that brought an end to the hauntings cannot be known and is not the important factor anyway. It also ended one of the most publicized hauntings of our times. What is important, though, is that the sightings did end so we can only hope and pray *that the souls are finally set free and are at peace.*

[Author's note: For a more detailed account on the crash and psychic phenomena that followed, I would recommend reading the book The Ghost of Flight 401 *by John G. Fuller.]*

Shadow Sphere

Throughout time, there have been many reports and writings on so-called *shadow phantoms.* In my previous book as in this book, a friend and I, as well as the couple written about in chapter one, witnessed such an entity in the guise of a hooded monk. This entity, as many other reports indicate, possesses a consciousness and is often attempting to impart some message or wisdom. This was certainly the case with the hooded monk seen by my friend, the couple and myself. Hooded monks are the most commonly reported phenomena. However, there are reports by people who saw regular bodily shapes, except they appeared as shadows. Some of them appeared to possess consciousness. In some cases, they appeared to be attempting to communicate and in other cases, they seemed to be simply observing as if out of curiosity. In still other cases, the shadows appeared on the walls simply going through normal routines, taking no notice of the people present. There are so many accounts of people who have been visited by what appeared to be shadow phantoms that it has become a phenomenon that is hard to deny. Certainly Liz Anderson would never deny it. She states the following, "It was the middle of the night. This would have been on a Tuesday. My husband was in Montreal, Quebec, on a business trip. He was not expected back until Thursday. Naturally, the lights were out. There was only slight illumination from the streetlights.

"I don't know what woke me. I just felt a chill and this undeniable presence. I sat up in bed fearing someone had broken into the room, and saw this shadow figure. His stature was the same as my husband's. I assumed he had arrived home early and did not turn the lights on so as not to disturb me. It was so real to me that I even told him he need not try to get ready for bed in the dark. I was awake but I received no reply. This confused me. Time seemed to speed up while I wondered why he was not even responding to me. Odder still, he was reaching out toward me.

"I panicked, this time convinced that a man had broken into the house. We had been hearing about many such home invasions taking place in Toronto of late. I began to tremble and felt icy cold as I reached for the bedside table light and phone. Then, suddenly, a feeling of warmth and comfort came over me and as I reached for the phone, I felt a warm hand cover my hand. Then I heard the voice of my husband say quite clearly, 'It is going to be all right, Izzy.' That was his pet name for me. No one else would know that. When I turned the light on, the shadow figure of what I now knew to be that of my husband vanished in the light. My trembling had stopped and I was no longer chilled. In fact, I was now feeling rather hot.

"Not three seconds went by when the phone rang. When you get a call in the middle of the night, a person is usually very worried, expecting bad news, but I was unusually calm. It was a hospital in Montreal informing me that my husband had suffered a heart attack. I was certainly upset by this news but there remained in me a prevailing, inner calm that he would be all right.

I flew to Montreal on the next available flight. He had already had surgery and came through it with flying colours. He was warned about his cholesterol and advised in no uncertain terms to lose weight and cut back on his workload. I had been urging him to do this for quite some time now. After all, he was not getting any younger and was a real workaholic, feeling he had to keep up with the younger members of the firm.

"Thankfully, he followed the doctor's advice. He began exercising, changed his diet and cut his hours, which included not travelling so much. The heart attack saved his life because if he had of continued on with that lifestyle, it would have been much worse and chances are he might not have made it. Still, I do not understand what happened that evening — how he was able to come to me. It certainly saved my sanity. I would have been in such a panic, I may have had a heart attack myself! Even though I don't understand, I just thank God he appeared. As a result of that visit, I just knew he was not going to die. That visit was for me, a blessing and even a miracle."

There is no set rule dictating how a ghost should appear. In the previous case, this is often referred to as a *phantom of the living* or *a crisis apparition*. The man was, after all, in a state between life and death. Although he was not yet pronounced clinically dead, he was well on his way out. He knew the hospital would contact his next of kin, in this case, his wife, but he also innately knew that he was going to live so he wanted to assure his wife of this. Thus, he may have astral projected. This could be one explanation for some of these shadow phantoms; those deceased or in between the state of life and death but cannot fully manifest. The other possible explanation is that they are at too great a distance from this earthly plane to appear in their solid, more familiar life form. In other words, they are fading into the other state of being. As in the first case, they could also be projected events from the past.

The most common shadow figures are the hooded monks. As stated before, they seem to have a tremendous, higher sentience, often omniscient. They are sometimes referred to as "interdimensional beings" that is, not of this world and as existing on a higher plane or dimension than the living. They are thought of as spirit guides or sages. They often appear unnoticed and silently observe, guide, and protect us. Others speculate that they are observing us to learn so as best to know how to guide us. This is not so different from the notion of so-called "guardian angels," although hooded monks are not as connected to us personally as are guardian angels who come to us, as legend and stories have it, at times of crisis. The monks come and go by their own mysterious volition and purpose.

I don't know who or what these hooded monks are, but I have interviewed many people who have encountered them and only twice was it a negative experience. In both these cases, the injuries sustained were due to panic as a result of running, causing personal injury. Interestingly, they healed more quickly and with less pain than would normally be expected.

In my own personal case, I feel the appearance of the monk was positive, as well as being a guide and omen for me. I felt he was trying to impart some wisdom on me or deliver a message. This is true of the other people I have interviewed who have also had visits from the monks. However, as was in my case, the initial reaction of fear or being startled seems to break the link or "connection" with them before their purpose becomes known to us. Then there is one version of the hooded monk as a harbinger of death as in the following case:

When the Grim Reaper Comes a Knocking?

Throughout this manuscript you have encountered reports of the elusive and mysterious Hooded Monk on numerous occasions. Up until October of 2006, I had never received any personal accounts that I could investigate or verify, although I have received numerous accounts of his appearance from various parts of the world. I will recount some of them but I always prefer to perform an on-site field investigation where I can get to know the environment and the people. Circumstantially, that is not always a viable option. However, one case that really caught my attention happened to be closer to home. It occurred in Fenelon Falls, which is a small town in central Ontario.

One stormy winter night, a woman went to answer her doorbell. She was alone in the house with her children. Her husband was at a bar with some friends. When she opened the door, she was greeted by the figure of what she assumed by its stature to be a male in a cape and hood. *Could it be the Hooded Monk all the way up in Fenelon Falls?* Nothing of a supernatural nature even crossed her mind at the time. She assumed that due to the weather, he was well covered up and was having car trouble or had been in an accident. She inquired if he was all right and turned toward the phone, asking him if he wanted her to call for help. When she turned her head back to the door anticipating a reply, he was simply gone! She stepped outside of the house and upon looking around, saw no signs of a car and no footprints in the freshly fallen snow. She was confused and astonished to say the least.

Shortly thereafter, another knock came on the door. This time it was the police informing her that her husband had been shot to death while trying to break up a fight in the bar he was at. Was this one of the hooded monks or a harbinger of death? The hooded monks always appear in the same form, at least as far as my research has indicated, but they serve different purposes. The ones that have appeared on Merion Street were not harbingers of death but in this case and similar others that I have come across, shortly after their appearance, news of a death follows. It can surely be no coincidence that for many decades now, the Grim Reaper has been depicted as a hooded spectre, though unlike the others unassociated with death, this entity is holding a scythe. In the case just cited, the hooded figure was not holding a scythe but his appearance and the subsequent news of her husband's murder strikes one as being something beyond mere coincidence. Throughout the ages, there have been numerous accounts of portents of death. Being no stranger to paranormal activity, looking back on the event the woman considered if this was a portent of death. Whether it was an unconscious projection or an actual visitation, it had the effect of bracing her for bad news so she would not fall apart, which is good since she had children to think of.

Still, hooded monks remain a mystery. Are they sages who were actually living beings at one time and advanced to a higher plane after death? This would certainly fit with the Buddhist philosophy in which we progress from the lower to more advanced states of consciousness, as well as there being different levels or "planes" of existence. The evolution is a type of self-transcendence where we lose our limited sense of self and reality and no longer identify ourselves by our bodies, jobs, belongings, etc., which in many Eastern traditions are thought of as not only being illusions but entrapments. Sometimes, our consciousness becomes in sync with higher or lower levels of existence, as everything is energy that vibrates at different energy frequencies yet exists simultaneously. These are those moments of enlightenment (the psychic Julian addressed this more thoroughly in Chapter 1 of this book). This also complements theories in quantum physics.

Still, others feel some of these shadow figures, including hooded monks, are ghostly manifestations of a negative nature. Perhaps that is true in some cases but as I said, they are the most common form of "shadow apparitions" and are generally positive and benevolent. With that being said, there are more and more reports being received by research centres and paranormal groups everyday. Perhaps they went unreported because being shadows, people merely dismissed them as imaginary. There are other shadow figures that are in a class of their own, unrelated to hooded monks.

Such is the case of the man who suffered a heart attack and then appeared in shadow form, which was most likely a *crisis apparition,* which is very different from a shadow figure. On the evening of January 17, 2001, Mrs. Margaret Bennet of Windsor, Ontario, went to bed at her usual time, which was around 10:00 p.m. She had trouble falling asleep that night, which was unusual for her. As a rule, she usually dropped right off, not even waking when her husband, Ron, would come to bed an hour or two later. Ron was a sales representative and travelled quite a bit, including crossing the border into the United States. On this particular day, Margaret had a very bad feeling about his leaving and asked him if he could not put this trip off for even a day as the weather was very bad. The snow was heavy, the winds gusty — causing whiteouts — and the roads were slippery. He shrugged all this off and tried to reassure her by reminding her that he had been on hundreds of trips in all kinds of weather, even worse than this. It was what he did for a living and she should be used to it after all these years. She countered, saying that throughout all these years, she had never had such a feeling of foreboding. He said, "Listen, honey, I have never even been in so much as a fender bender." She failed to persuade him otherwise, so he left at 10:00 a.m. that morning, saying he would call her as soon as he reached the hotel room. At the door, he turned to kiss her goodbye and seeing that she looked very disconcerted, gave her a warm hug and said, "I promise you I *will come home*." She was very anxious all day. She cleaned the house from top to bottom just to keep busy. She didn't want to be away from the phone so she didn't even leave the house. By 11:00 p.m., when she had still not heard from him, she was frantic. She even had two drinks to calm herself, which is very unlike her. She was strictly a social drinker. It did make her drowsy enough that, portable phone in hand, she turned on the television and lay down on the couch. She must have dropped off to sleep out of sheer exhaustion because the next thing she knew, her husband gently shook her by the shoulder then stood back, looking down at her, smiling. She propped herself up on her elbow, trying to clear her head and said, "Oh, thank God you decided to come home." He replied, "I told you I would come home." He no sooner uttered those words when the phone rang, causing her to almost jump out of her skin. The phone had gotten underneath her so she turned away from him to retrieve it while glancing at the clock on the wall. It was 1:47 a.m. Who could be calling at this hour? Her heart sank. It was the police informing her that her husband had been involved in an accident and that a cruiser was on its way over. She said that they must have the wrong person because her husband was right here, but when she looked over to where he had been standing, he was no longer there. She then knew that they did not have the wrong person. Fighting back tears, she asked where he was and if he was all right. They would not answer any of her questions. They would only calmly assure her that a cruiser would be there any minute. She refused to believe this was happening but knew that her husband was dead. She could hold back the tears no longer and with shaking hands, called her sister and half-hysterically blurted out that Ron was dead and the police were on their way over. Her sister was in shock almost shouted, "What? Never mind. I'm on my way over." She lived close by and arrived only a few minutes after the police. It was true. Her husband had been killed in a five-car pileup involving one snowplow. For some reason, even though they were very close, it was several months before she told her sister about her ominous feelings regarding the trip and that before the police called, not only had her husband appeared to her, he had actually touched her. She added rather sadly that his last words to her were that *he promised he would be home. He kept his promise.* He had come home, if only in spirit. His appearance provided her with comfort because she figures if he could appear to her in spirit form that means there is life after death and he is with her still.

A Not So Urban Legend

We have all heard stories that are repeated, sometimes through generations. They seem to take on a life of their own. They are commonly referred to as *urban legends.* I am referring to such stories as the couple who, returning home from a date, runs out of gas in a secluded area. The boyfriend dutifully goes off, gas can in hand, to the nearest gas station while the girlfriend remains alone in the car.

What seems like an unreasonable amount of time passes by and she becomes quite anxious. Not soon after, she becomes aware of this strange swaging, dragging noise emanating from the roof of the car. Just as she is about to go out and investigate, a police car with its lights flashing comes up behind the stranded vehicle. She responds with both fear and relief.

It turns out that the police are scouting the area for a man who has escaped from a maximum-security prison for the "criminally insane."

One of the officers knocks on the passenger side of the door and tells her that it's best that she remain in the car. Panicked, she does not comply and upon emerging from the car, is greeted by the horrific sight of her dead boyfriend hanging upside down from a tree branch, gently swaying to and fro. His throat had been cut. Perhaps the moral of this story is to always comply with police requests or keep spare gas in the car!

There is also the one about a babysitter receiving threatening phone calls throughout the evening. She is alone in the house and throughout the evening grows more and more frightened. She can finally stand it no more and phones the police. When they get back to her after tracing the calls, they tell her in no uncertain terms to get out of the house *now*. The threatening calls were coming from within the house! All of her roommates had not really left. In fact, they were all still home but had all been murdered. (You may have seen the movie based on this legend entitled *Black Christmas*.)

The Long Road Home

One of the most persistent and intriguing stories is that of disappearing hitchhiker. As legend has it, an unsuspecting driver stops to offer a ride to a young woman in apparent distress. She is often in a party dress and is sometimes wet and distraught in appearance. The driver offers the woman a jacket, which she readily accepts. The driver is concerned that the young woman has suffered some kind of trauma, perhaps an accident or even a rape. She merely stares ahead, not muttering a word except for her destination. The driver takes her to her destination but neglects to retrieve his jacket. He therefore returns to the address the following day to get his garment. A woman, maybe in her sixties, greets him at the door. She is dismayed and somewhat saddened to hear his strange tale. She requests that he wait and a moment later, returns with a picture of a young woman of about nineteen years of age. She is smiling and is dressed in party attire. The man immediately recognizes her as the woman he drove home the previous evening. The woman nods and explains that this has happened before. She goes on to explain that the young woman he brought to this address was her daughter and that she had been killed on her way home from her prom in a car accident some thirty years ago. The anniversary of her death was the previous night. She has apparently been trying to get home ever since.

Of course, the man cannot believe his ears. The woman says she understands his disbelief but if he would like proof, he can go to her grave, and gives him directions.

The man is so caught up in this fantastic story that he does indeed go to the gravesite. Not only does he find her grave, but also, neatly folded, on the tombstone is his jacket!

A variation of this story has the man driving a young woman to an address that turns out to be a cemetery. The man turns to ask the woman if she was sure she had the right address or perhaps he heard her wrong. The woman simply smiles, exits the car and vanishes into the cemetery.

Urban legends usually evolve from an event that actually took place. They no doubt become embellished over years of retelling.

Photo courtesy of Dale Kaczmarek of the Ghost Research Society

"Home." Resurrection Cemetery. Chicago, Illinois. Home and focal point of the infamous Resurrection Mary, the most well known of the so-called "vanishing hitchhikers."

Such is the case with the most famous of the disappearing hitchhiker stories; that of Resurrection Mary, so named because the location this woman asks to be taken to is that of Resurrection Cemetery. It is located at 7600 Archer Avenue in Chicago, Illinois. This particular vanishing hitchhiker is purportedly the ghost of a young Polish woman returning home from a dance at a place then known as the O'Henry Ballroom (now called the Willowbrook Ballroom). The dance took place back in the 1930s. Her name was Mary Bregovy. She had blond hair and striking blue eyes. She apparently got into a very heated argument with her escort/boyfriend and got out of the car, intending to walk home. Alas, she never made it because she was struck and killed by a hit-and-run driver. She, like the other ghostly hitchhikers, has been trying to get home in vain ever since. Mary is often spotted walking down Archer Avenue. She is hard to miss because she is very beautiful and dressed in a strikingly white party gown. She is almost luminescent. Sometimes she just walks, while other times she attempts to get a ride. Some people who have passed her and looked back to get a look at her face swear she didn't have one. In place of a face is a black void (that is one sure sign that you are seeing a ghost). This was the case one early evening when a couple was driving home and the wife noticed a woman slowly making her way down Archer Avenue. Curious, she turned around as they passed her; she saw the figure of the woman in a white gown but in place of a face was a black space and nothing else. She was so frightened that she did not tell her husband to stop to investigate, but ordered him to speed up. She did not dare look back again. He asked her what was wrong but she had to wait until her shaking subsided in order to explain to him what she had just witnessed. Another intriguing manifestation about Mary is that there is a section of the iron gates that are bent as though by human hands, which is attributed to Mary. A very rare occurrence, indeed, as the manipulation or even destruction of the physical environment is usually but not always associated with poltergeist phenomena, not ghosts.

I was thrilled when I got the opportunity to interview a man who had had an actual personal encounter with Mary. We will call him Archie. He is a retired engineer and resides with his wife in Chicago. He does not

Photo courtesy of Dale Kaczmarek of the Ghost Research Society

Bent bars on the gates of Resurrection Cemetery, where imprints of human fingers can be seen.

want his real name used because, as he laughingly puts it, "My family might try to have me put away."

This event took place in March of 1967. While driving down Archer Avenue, Archie came upon this lovely, young woman slowly walking down the avenue in a party dress that was pure white and rather flimsy; he was amazed that she had no coat on. Thinking she was in some sort of shock or trouble, he pulled over and asked her if she was in need of assistance. She smiled and slowly glided into the car. She gave him the address to which she wanted to be taken. He became confused when, upon arriving at the address she had given to him, they were outside the front gates of Resurrection Cemetery. He turned to her and said, "I'm sorry, miss. I must have taken a wrong turn. You certainly can't live here." She turned to him, smiled sweetly and left the car. He watched in shock and amazement as she passed right through the locked gates!

He sat there for a good fifteen minutes, not believing his eyes and seriously questioning his sanity. Even though the heater was on full, he felt chilled to the bone. He finally composed himself and headed home. When he entered the house, his wife asked him what was wrong, as he was silent and pale. Ironically, she said that *he looked as though he had seen a ghost.* He looked startled by her comment but silently nodded, grunting a barely audible, "Uh, huh." In a somewhat shaky voice, he tried to put his condition down to it having been a long day and a tricky ride home due to the snow. He did not sleep that night. It was at least a month before he finally shared the truth with her. She didn't know what to make of the strange tale but cautioned him to keep the story to himself, which he fully intended to. That is, until now.

I asked him why he kept the story to himself for so long. He replied with the common refrain that he was afraid people would think he was crazy or as he put it, "one card short of a deck." I asked him what effect, if any, this experience had had on him. He replied that for quite some time, he was in complete disbelief but that "denial can only take you so far and then you have to face the facts and accept the truth even if you don't understand it. I've never been a religious, church-going man. I believe in God but was never sure about life after death. Who can be? I think it's really a matter of faith. But this experience changed that for me. I now do believe there is life after death; that something of us goes on after we die. However, I was a bit confused and bothered about the notion of 'heaven' and being reunited with our loved ones. I don't like to think that we just go wandering around old haunts. I feel a bit sad for this individual. Maybe it only happens to some people for whatever reason. I don't understand it. It's all a bit too deep and philosophical for me to get my head around. On the other hand, maybe I shouldn't feel sad for Mary because in a way, she could be doing what, in a way, we are all trying to do; just trying to get home." Let us hope and pray she makes it home someday. She has wandered for far too long.

[Author's note: The story of Resurrection Mary was originally supposed to have been in my first book but when the publishers received the manuscript, Mary had disappeared. All they had was the photograph of the cemetery and were disappointed that there was no story to go along with the picture. I only hope that when the publisher receives this manuscript, Mary is with the rest of the manuscript this time!]

"Why Shouldn't There Be Ghosts?" The Adventures of Carl Jung

In my previous book *True Tales of the Paranormal,* I wrote about the paranormal experiences that Carl Jung (1875–1961) had and how this impacted on his relationship with Sigmund Freud, who believed and supported the supernatural more than he let be known publicly. In fact, Freud was a member of the British Society of Psychical Research. He tended to distance himself from such research as he already had a reputation as being a bit of an eccentric, no doubt due to his interest in the paranormal. Still, being of scientific mind, he held on to the belief that eventually "supernatural" phenomena would eventually be explained in logical, naturalistic terms. Yet he had no doubt that mental telepathy was not only a certain possibility but that it took place more commonly than recognized, but only under certain conditions. Freud was a brilliant man so it is a shame that he did not pursue further research in this area out of fear for his reputation as a "serious" scientist. In fact, toward the end of his life, he expressed just such a regret. He spoke more openly of it and said that he wished he had examined it more closely. Perhaps being so ill with cancer and coming close to death, he was giving such phenomena deeper consideration.

Dr. Jung, on the other hand, was not so overly concerned with his reputation or what the scientific community thought of him. His ardent interest in the paranormal was no doubt in part a result of his numerous personal experiences, which are well documented. What I neglected to include in my book, however, was a fascinating and terrifying experience that Dr. Jung had in the 1920s. He was visiting London, England, to deliver a series of lectures. Friends had rented him a cottage in Buckinghamshire. It was not a pleasant experience. He slept poorly (when he slept at all) due to various unusual disturbances. The first manifestation was that that of a sickly, sweet odour that permeated the entire bedroom. In spite of opening the windows, he was unable to dispel the odour. He was further disturbed by the persistent sound of water dripping, in spite of the fact that he was nowhere near a tap, nor was it raining. The source of the dripping sound remained a mystery.

On another occasion, he became agitated by more odd sounds such as rustling coming from a corner of the bedroom, as well as cracking noises resounding from the furniture. He also heard what sounded like something brushing up against the walls even though he was alone in the room.

His most frightening experience by far took place on his fifth visit to this residence. Just as he was falling off to sleep, his attention was drawn to the pillow next to him. To his shock and horror, he saw the hideous face of an old woman. Half of her face was gone and the one eye she did have was wide open and glaring right at him! He leapt out of bed and spent the remainder of the night sitting in an armchair with the lights on. From then on, he stayed in another room where he found he was free from any other "disturbances." Jung was not alone in his experiences. Everyone who had stayed in that room felt the same fear and shared similar experiences.

To round off his considerable experiences with the paranormal and altered states of consciousness, in 1944 Jung had a near-death experience after suffering a heart attack. To quote from the book *The Encyclopedia of Ghosts and Spirits* by Rosemary Ellen Guiley: "As he lay in bed, a nurse saw him surrounded by a bright halo of light, something she had observed around patients who where dying. Jung, however, recovered from the heart attack and later recounted what happened to him. Characteristically, his experience was laden with mythic imagery. He felt himself to be floating high above Earth, became aware that he was leaving it and then saw near him a huge block of stone, which had been hollowed out to form a temple. He knew that he was expected inside the temple, and as he drew closer to it, his earthly desires and attitudes fell away and awareness dawned that inside he would come to understand the meaning of his life. At that moment, however, his earthly doctor appeared in the form of the Basileus of Kos, the healer at the temple of Aeculapius, the Roman god of healing, telling him he must return to Earth. Jung did so, though reluctantly, and with great resentment toward the doctor."[1]

The poor doctor must have been confused by this reaction; after all, most people would have an attitude of gratitude toward the man who had just saved his life but Jung was not like most people. And his near-death experience was not like most other NDEs. But then again it is what one would expect from a person like Dr. Carl Gustav Jung, who has left a tremendous and lasting legacy; whose work, theories, and principles have influenced many diverse disciplines and clinical/research work such as psychoanalysis, many types of literature, religious studies (both Western and Eastern), and even physics, quantum mechanics, and of course, parapsychology. I wonder if books such as *Mysticism and the New Physics* by Michael Talbot would have ever been written without the pioneer work done by Jung. Jung published an intriguing and thought-provoking book in 1978 entitled *Psychology and the Occult,* which is well worth reading, along with his many other books and papers exploring the paranormal and psychology. His theory and principles on synchronicity have entered many cultural mainstreams in his writings on precognitive dreams (in fact, three days before his own death, Jung had a dream that he interpreted as a portent of his own passing, which turned out to be true). He also believed in reincarnation, like over half the population of the earth does, but he did not believe he was here to resolve karmic debt but rather, to fulfill a destiny for mankind, which he had grave concerns over. One of the most inspiring and intriguing things he said (at least for me) was that he *believed his work would serve to prove that the essence of God existed in everyone.*

Right Number — Wrong Time?

Steve Patterson retired to bed early on April 20, 2004. He was feeling exhausted and slightly chilled. He put it down to all the preparations he and his brother had been busily engaged in for the past five months in preparation for their parents' fiftieth wedding anniversary. Andrew was two years older than Steve and his only sibling. Even though they were very different and their lives had taken different paths (Steve was a lawyer whereas Andrew was a writer and an artist) they had remained close throughout their lives and were both very devoted to their parents, Martin and Catherine.

The brothers' preparations for this special occasion had been painstakingly meticulous. With the difference in their personalities, there had been some disagreements on the arrangements but their cousin, Debbie, who was like a sister to them and had been a tremendous help through it all, would step in and settle any disagreements they were having. It was all worth it, though, because the party was as close to perfect as anyone could hope to get. A good time was had by all and the guests of honour were touched beyond words.

When it was all over Steve was not the only one who would be going to bed early that night. He and his brother hugged each other goodbye as they prepared to leave their parents' home, and Debbie gave them both a hard pat on their backs. Steve told them both that he was going straight home and would call in a couple of days when he "woke up," then said to his brother, "You look like you could use some serious sleep yourself, mate. Are you all right?"

Before Andrew had a chance to reply, Debbie added, "You look more than just tired. You're sweating and you look kind of pale and pasty. There is a flu going about." She even put her hand on his cheek and forehead.

Andrew assured them that he was perfectly fine, just very tired like all of them were. After a brief hesitation, Steve clutched Andrew's shoulder, saying, "OK, then. I'll call you in a couple of days and you be sure to hit the sheets as soon as you get home."

"I will, I will, and you be sure to do the same." With that, the two brothers went their separate ways into the cool, dark night. Debbie, still feeling uneasy about Andrew, told herself not to be such a mother hen and stayed behind to help her aunt and uncle.

Five days went by and Steve realized he had not yet talked to his brother and parents or Debbie, either, who had certainly been right about a flu going around. He had been more than just tired. When he woke late the next morning, he was feverish, sweating, and aching from head to toe. He thought Andrew had probably had the flu as well, which explained his appearance after the party. He felt like he should call him but could simply not muster the strength. He basically just remained in bed for a few days until he was finally able to get and stay up for more than just a few minutes. While he was getting down some tea, toast, and juice, the compulsion to call his brother was growing stronger and stronger. He didn't understand this strange sense of urgency. As he recalls it, "It was as though Andrew would be catching a plane pretty soon and if I didn't call now, I would miss him."

He swallowed down the last bit of his juice, grabbed the portable phone and, flopping down on the sofa, proceeded to call Andrew.

Andrew didn't answer immediately, but more unusual, the answering machine didn't kick in as it should have on the fourth ring. Steve called again, this time manually, instead of pressing the speed dial, thinking he had probably hit the wrong button. He pressed the numbers carefully and once again, the phone rang a good eight or nine times before Steve hung up. He looked at the phone in utter confusion, wondering "what the hell was going on." He sat up and redialed with some determination. This time, Andrew picked up on the second ring. Steve felt a sense of immediate relief upon hearing the sound of his brother's voice. He said, "Hey, Andrew, it's good to hear your voice. There's either something wrong with my phone or your answering machine is off. This is the third time I've tried to get through."

His brother replied, "It's good to hear your voice, too. I'm glad you got through."

"Me, too. Sorry I didn't call earlier in the week but Deb was right about that flu. I've been in bed all week. How about you? Did you get nailed by it, too, 'cause you sure looked like you were coming down with something."

Andrew replied, "Yeah, it got me *real* good. Never been so sick in my life. *But it's all over now*. In fact I've never felt better in my entire life."

"That's great," Steve said. "What did you take for it?"

"Actually, I didn't have to take anything at all. I just went to sleep and that was it."

"Well, good for you. You certainly sound bright and cheery. Me, I'm still recuperating a bit, but certainly much better than I have been. That was quite a celebration we pulled off, huh?"

The conversation went on like that for a few more minutes before the brothers hung up. The only odd thing that caught Steve's attention was that when he said to Andrew that they would get together real soon, his brother replied, "Well, I can't make any promises." Steve just thought he was joking, but looking back on it now it made perfect sense and even gives him a bit of a chill. Steve also noticed that Andrew sounded very mellow and spacey, like he had taken a tranquilizer or something. He just put it down to his brother's weakened state, even if he did insist that he was fully recovered.

A short while after speaking with Andrew, Steve received a call from Debbie. She sounded very strange and he immediately asked her

135

what was wrong. She said that she was so sorry. They had just found out themselves. By now, Steve was quite agitated and impatient, insisting that she tell him what was going on.

She said that she had gone over to Andrew's because they had made arrangements to get together on this day unless one of them cancelled. She found him dead, in bed. In fact, he was still in his clothes, as though he had just collapsed there. The police were on the way but by her own observations, he had been dead at least a couple of days.

Steve was shocked to say the least. He practically yelled in protest that that was impossible, adding, "What the hell are you talking about? I was just talking to him not fifteen minutes ago!"

She gently replied that that could not be due to the condition of the body and the somewhat obvious fact that the phone had been knocked off the hook. Probably by Andrew himself when he fell into bed. He had probably fainted or was trying to call for help and dropped the phone.

Steve just could not believe his ears. He felt the room begin to spin around him as though he were in some kind of dream. No, a nightmare, yet there would be no denying it.

A few days later, it was confirmed that Andrew had died approximately three days before the phone call the two brothers had shared. The last phone call they would ever share. Thinking back on the conversation, some of the things Steve took as a bit odd made eerie sense now. The statement that it "got him really good," emphasizing the word "really," and that bit about getting together but not making any promises. Also, the clincher that "it was all over now" instead of saying "I feel better now." He was in shock. He wished he had said more; kept him on the phone longer. You never know when you are talking to someone that it may be the last conversation you will ever have with them. He thought with deep sorrow that *we take far too much for granted in this life*. He vowed to change that and secretly hoped that, somehow, he could talk to his brother again. Although he felt silly doing so, he even dialed Andrew's number. *The line was dead*. In this case, it offered the surviving brother just that and assured most people that part of us does go on when our physical self dies. As well, most of those I have spoken to not only share his sentiment, but consider it a blessing, especially when you take into consideration how often a loved one dies suddenly and we never even have the chance to say goodbye or I love you. Quite a gift from beyond.

Why do such things happen to a select number of people and not everybody? I can only speculate that either the deceased is unable to make contact as they may have crossed way over into "the light" or that the survivors would not benefit from such a call, perhaps making things more painful, unbelievable (rendering the death harder to accept because, after all, they had spoken to the so-called deceased on the phone!), and preventing people to let go and allow the healing and grieving process to begin. I should add that with all the technology we have, such contact with the dead is not limited to the phone. I have heard reports of contact from the deceased via the television, computers, and even text messages. Considering that all is energy, which as you recall never dies but merely changes form, it is almost logical that the deceased would employ energy-based technology to reach out and touch someone.

A Watery Grave

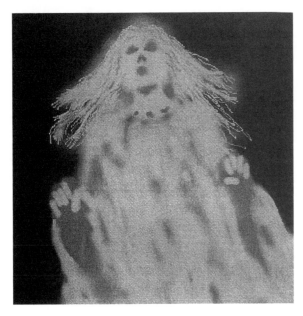

"Ghost Girl." The spirit of the dead girl of Lafontaine.

In the summer of 1959, the body of a young woman washed up on the shore of Georgian Bay in the area of Lafontaine. In actuality, the body was not found on the shore but wedged in amongst the rocks at a part of the shoreline where people do not normally swim because of all the rocks. It is a beautiful, rather posh area with high-priced, luxury homes, many of them vacant throughout most of the year. It could be considered a place for the "privileged class" who like to keep up appearances ... which sometimes meant keeping many skeletons securely locked away in their respective closets. Such was the case in the 1950s when the young daughter of one of these part-time residents committed pregnancy without benefit of marriage. This was considered unacceptable by some members of society in those days, especially amongst this class of people. In the 1950s, especially in some segments of society, it was considered a complete and utter disgrace that could not only be ruinous to the woman's life and future prospects, but to the family's reputation, as well.

There are two variations in relation to the origin of this haunting. One has it that it was the wife of a steel mogul from Hamilton, Ontario, who became pregnant as a result of an extramarital affair. It was said that she met an untimely death due to a botched abortion, which her husband had forced her to have. Her lifeless and rather blood-depleted body was disposed of in the waters of Georgian Bay to hide this shame.

The second version is the more plausible one. It is certainly easier to verify but still difficult due to the lack of official, in-depth reporting and possible cover-ups. I have had to rely on sketchy, shallow records and good, old-fashioned gossip that has survived the times, as well as the psychic that the surviving sister consulted, who offered invaluable insight.

The young victim was Katherine Mitchell. She was fifteen years of age, just approaching sixteen. She was a lovely-looking young woman with blond hair and large, almost luminous blue eyes. She and her family had been summering in Lafontaine since she was five. She had one other sibling, Margaret, aged eighteen. Margaret would prove to be a vital element in the illumination of the untold story. I had the fortunate opportunity to interview her on June 7, 2005. She now resides in Toronto and is married with four children. She remains haunted by the death of her sister and admits to, at one time, having very strong feelings against her father, mother, and the one she refers to as the right hand of her sister's (along with her unborn child's) demise, calling him "that dreadful, snivelling Mathew." She held lingering anger against her parents because they refused to ever discuss the death and had been far too strict. If they had been more approachable in times of trouble, she thought that the entire tragedy may have been averted.

Author: Thank you for meeting with me. I'm sure this must be very strange coming out of the blue like this after so many years.

Margaret: I always welcome the opportunity to talk about my sister. It was so senseless and needless.

Author: You've heard the stories of her haunting the part of the beach …

Margaret: Where her body was found? [Smiling and nodding] Yes, I've heard them all.

Author: Do you believe them?

Margaret: Well, although I have never believed in such things before, I am inclined to believe some of the stories. It distressed me, the thought of my sister not being at rest, so I hoped they were not true, but I felt they were. That would mean that she is stuck haunting the place where she died while those responsible apparently lived happily ever after.

Author: So what is the story?

Margaret: My sister informed me that she had become pregnant by this cad, Mathew. I warned her about him. He denied being the father but he knew full well that he was the only one she was seeing. We lived very sheltered lives. Our parents were very strict, especially about our comings and goings. Because he is from a so-called "good" family, they trusted her to be with him to go swimming and such. In fact, they had hoped that the relationship would eventually lead to marriage, but that is not something Mathew had in mind. To him, she was just a plaything. He had his eyes and plans on another girl back in the city. My sister knew nothing of this and when I told her, she refused to believe me. He was a calculating, manipulative person and figured his prospects would be better with the other girl. He was a cold, slick player, out for only himself. I wouldn't put anything beyond him if it meant getting what he wanted. A pregnancy or even word of an abortion *would not be good for him* and would certainly ruin any plans he had with his girlfriend in the city.

One afternoon, they went swimming, but she never came home. My parents phoned the family, who also had a vacation home not far from ours. Mathew had been home for at least three hours and swore they had left at the same time. When she had still not returned by the evening, my parents called the police. They questioned Mathew, our family, and combed the beach and waters as best they could but it was dark so they would have to resume their search the next morning. Her body was eventually found wedged in some boulder-like rocks on the shoreline at a part of the beach where none of us ever swam because it was too rocky. It was assumed that she drowned, even though Mathew said they had left together. Then he changed his story, saying that she must have gone back in for another swim. Even if she had done so, she wouldn't have been swimming in that part of the lake. It's even hard to get to as you have to make your way over so many of these huge rocks, which she wouldn't chance out of concern for the baby.

It didn't make any sense. And then there was the timing. She had already confided in me that she was pregnant and that she was going to tell Mathew. She was thinking they could get married early. She really had it bad for him. I told her she was deluding herself; that was not going to happen. She got angry and stormed out of the room, saying I didn't know him like she did. He loved her and would do the right thing. He did the right thing, all right; the right thing for himself. I firmly believe that he drowned her. Knowing him as I did, he is capable of anything. He also did not seemed to be genuinely grieved; it was a strained, appropriate acting job that he didn't even bother to keep up for that long. He certainly didn't look grieved at the funeral. In fact, his appearance was more that of impatience and discomfort. And besides, I cannot see my sister drowning. She has been swimming since before she could almost walk. She took to the water like a fish. Nevertheless, the cause of death was put down as drowning.

She had what was called a blunt force blow on the back of her head, but they attributed that to her crashing into the rocks where her body was found. How awful, found wedged between rocks. I know he either took her to that place under the pretense that they could have more privacy, and then struck her on the head with a rock or he actually got into the water and physically drowned her. There is absolutely no proof of this, so what could I do? I did confront him once but he just said that I was crazy and if I dared to spread such stories, he would have me up on defamation charges. I found it interesting and telling that he never went swimming in the lake again. In fact, after her death, he never joined his family at the vacation home again.

Now I am not a hundred percent sure about all this paranormal stuff, though I do believe that something of us continues on after we die. I consulted a psychic who had an excellent reputation. She confirmed what I had suspected. She told me that he had taken her to this secluded part of the beach and struck her on the back of the head with a rock. It was not a fatal blow but enough to render her unconscious. I figured it was his way because he is too much of a coward to actually get into the water and drown her. Plus he himself may be injured or even drowned in the struggle instead of her. Lord knows he could not take such a chance. He then plunged her into the water where, being unconscious, she drowned. The tides took her out and then brought her back in.

I was distressed to hear from the psychic that her soul is not yet free, which is why I believe there may be something to the stories of her spirit being seen. As far as the police were concerned, it was an open-and-shut case. Mathew's family had considerable influence so the story was pretty much hushed up. There was a small mention of it in a few newspapers regarding the drowning of a fifteen-year-old girl in the Georgian Bay area of Lafontaine, and of course we made sure there was an extensive obituary including her picture, but that was the end of it. If these stories are true, maybe it's not the end of it. The psychic said I should pray daily for her soul and the psychic would do what she could to help guide the soul to the other side. I hope our actions were successful. I have not heard anything for several years about her being seen so maybe she is finally at rest.

I should add that I felt good about this psychic from the moment I met her. I have not been up to that place for eons as our family sold the house shortly after this incident. Yet she wanted to be as accurate as possible and insisted that she must be at or near the site that the tragedy took place. So the two of us drove up and without any help or guidance from me, she went right to the place where my sister's body was found. I stayed behind as I would never make it over those rocks, but I could see the psychic. After a while, I noticed that she seemed to be praying and then crying. She told me what I told you when we were halfway home. Up until then, she was completely quiet and seemed rather disturbed and sad. I was relieved to hear that my sister did not suffer, as she was unconscious. There was no panic or terror that a drowning person would likely experience. At least that's something. There was, however, an overwhelming sense of sadness, grief, and betrayal. She also sensed the emotions of confusion and being lost. One of the other things that convinced me that this woman was no charlatan was that she said my sister's right arm had been broken. When her body was found, it was in the rocks, actually more like small boulders, but her right arm had become wedged in between two of the boulders, which is what kept her body in that place. The psychic would have no way of knowing that. It was never reported.

Author: What are some of the stories you heard?

Margaret: Several people have reported seeing a young woman in a white robe (which she put on over her bathing suit after swimming) wandering slowly and aimlessly up and down the beach. They described her to a T. Her right arm was dangling as if broken and she had her left arm on her stomach or, at other times, the back of her head. Everyone who has seen her reported the same image even though these people did not know each other — we have a lot of tourists who rent places for a couple of weeks so they would not even have known about the drowning — and had not shared their experiences, so these were all independent witnesses. She was also dripping wet. Every time a witness would approach her, as she was obviously injured and in need of help, she would vanish.

Other times, this same girl, dripping wet in the white robe, would be seen standing on the boulders staring out over the bay. They would call out to her, asking if she was all right, but she took no notice of them so they just went about their business. The next time they looked over to where they had seen her, she was no longer there, yet no one had seen her walking up the path of the beach, which was the only way out.

I'm not sure about one of the strangest stories I heard because by this time, word had started to spread around the locals and you know how a story spreading gets embellished. There were two or three reports about swimmers feeling like something had taken hold of their ankles. It was a very firm grip. When they broke free, they swam as fast as they could to the shore and apparently refused to go in the water again. Now, whether it was seaweed or their imaginations, as the story was so well known by then, I don't know. I do know that my sister would not try to hurt or scare anyone. The theory was that she was reaching out for help. Maybe these people have been watching too many horror movies.

Author: Yes, as a story like this start to spread, it evolves into an urban legend.

Margaret: Exactly. Mind you, long after the story died down, tourists who knew nothing of such an old incident would report seeing her. The locals really didn't discuss it much but I had heard the odd rumour about suicide and even murder, but that seemed so far-fetched; things like that just don't happen to us, only "other" people in the news. It's a good thing we moved away as soon as we did. It took about a year for the house to sell but our family never returned. But, as I said earlier, besides the retelling of what is now an old story, I have heard only the odd report of her being sighted quite a while ago, so I can only hope and pray that she has moved on. The psychic has indicated that she senses she is at peace now. I am also happy to report that that cad's plans for marrying his little rich, well-connected girlfriend did not pan out — lucky for her. I often wonder if she suspected something. Lord knows, he got around and she must have found out about that.

My parents never spoke of it but when my first daughter was born and I named her Katherine, they were so thrilled. I was afraid that their doting over her so much might spoil her, but that didn't happen. She is a kind, loving, trusting, generous soul, much like my sister. And coincidently, she has blond hair and big blue eyes just like Katherine. How about that!

Author: Maybe it's more than a coincidence.

Margaret: [Laughing] You never know. She certainly has my sister's spirit and other characteristics, but she has always been terrified of the water. We have a pool and even as a baby she would cry if you brought her near it, which may suggest something. I just know she is a blessing to our family and has brought great joy to my parents. She seemed to breathe new life into them, as they were never the same after my sister's death until the baby came along.

Author: I would like to thank you once again for allowing me to interview you on what I'm sure is a painful subject.

Margaret: Not at all. I did it for my sister; anything to keep her story alive and hopefully shed some light on it.

Hotel Garry: Some Check In But Never Leave

The Fort Garry Hotel in Winnipeg, Manitoba, is a majestic structure of grand hotels built in days gone by. First constructed in 1913, it stands not far from where Upper Fort Garry was once located, which was built back in 1835 on the former site of one of the earliest trading posts in Manitoba. This is a hotel that is no stranger to history; therefore, it not surprising that it also has a reputation of being haunted. As you will read, this is a well-earned reputation. Even those who profess not to be in possession of even a smidgen of psychic ability nevertheless seem to automatically detect the presence of *unregistered guests*. Some are localized to specific places, like one particular elevator and a dining room. The other phenomena, for which there are numerous accounts all sharing similar occurrences, seem to be concentrated in room 202.

A Political Ghost of a Chance

Some interviews are harder to come by than others, such as when the people are in the public spotlight. Just as so many have expressed the sentiment that they never spoke of their paranormal experiences for fear of being ridiculed or thought of as being crazy, it can be that more challenging for people in certain professions such as law enforcement; judges, doctors, and politicians who, unlike the other aforementioned professions, must be elected against opponents. Anything can be used as fodder to discredit you or cast doubt on your competence. This can be especially true for public officials like politicians, and maybe even more so for women who may have made a good deal of political headway but still have a very long way to go and continue to be judged by a different standard than their male counterparts. Such is the case with the first woman in this section who recounted some unexplained and unusual experiences she had during her brief stay at the Fort Garry Hotel while on a political trip.

The woman I am referring to is Brenda Chamberlain. She is the federal Member of Parliament representing Guelph, Ontario (the riding where yours truly happens to reside). Her experiences were first brought to my attention in 2005 by someone else I know who works in the political arena. She wondered why I had never interviewed Mrs. Chamberlain about her experiences, considering I wrote about the paranormal and this lady was the MP for my city. The answer was that I had not been aware of her experiences at Fort Garry, though I was well acquainted with the paranormal activity associated with that particular hotel.

I wrote Mrs. Chamberlain, explaining to her that I was writing a sequel to a book on the paranormal and that someone had brought her experiences to my attention. In spite of her very demanding schedule, she responded to me by phone very shortly after receiving my correspondence. Although she seemed somewhat mystified as to why this story was still attracting periodic attention, she was very helpful and open with me, relating her brief but memorable experiences at the Fort Garry Hotel.

Mrs. Chamberlain was attending a Liberal Party caucus retreat in August of 2000. She was assigned to the rather infamous room 202. Unbeknownst to her at the time, this room has a well-known and well-deserved reputation for being haunted. I say well deserved because Mrs. Chamberlain is not the only one to have had encounters with a mysterious presence while residing in room 202.

Imagine if you will, going to bed for the evening in an unfamiliar hotel room and being woken up by the sensation of someone climbing into bed beside you! This is precisely what happened to Mrs. Chamberlain. She even felt the mattress shift! She says she that she is a light sleeper so she could not have possibly missed something as pronounced as that. Who could? Nevertheless, in a strange environment and being half-asleep, one would consider that they were merely dreaming. Only it happened a second time. This time, there was no question in her mind that she was wide awake. This was no dream. She found nothing amiss in her room, certainly not another person. She didn't know what to make of it. Considering this is a woman who is not scared off by a life of politics in Ottawa, it is no surprise that she was not scared off by this "unusual" event. In fact, she even managed to get some more sleep that night.

The following day, she jokingly mentioned her experience to a couple of other MPs (she even suggested to the then Prime Minister, Jean Chrétien, that she should only have to pay for half the room because she apparently had a roommate. He simply gave her a polite "no comment" sheepish smile). Others took it a bit more seriously, asking Mrs. Chamberlain if she was aware that the hotel was supposedly haunted. She had *not* been aware of this at all but soon learned of other stories that were in fact quite similar to her own. Mrs. Chamberlain also related to me that one fellow MP also had an unusual experience of her own.

As the MP was preparing to leave, she had taken special care to pack her cellphone, but, upon arriving at the airport, she was mystified to discover the phone was missing. She immediately contacted the hotel even though she was certain she had packed it (one tends to take special care with objects like cellphones and laptops).

After checking the room the MP had been in, they informed her that they had found the phone, and further stated that things go disappearing in that room all the time. As a matter of fact, I was informed by a staff member that things not only disappear around the hotel all the time, but often turn up in odd places like the kitchen freezer.

It's been a few years since these events and although Mrs. Chamberlain has suggested that she does not believe in ghosts, her experience at the Fort Garry Hotel has obviously left a lasting impression on her, and to this day, the events do not appear to have any logical explanation (besides, who is to say that the paranormal is not logical; it's just not well understood yet). The same is true of other events that people have had at this hotel that have no logical explanation. I interviewed a man in March of 2004 who was in Manitoba on a business trip. He was very tired and this was to be his last night before returning to his home in Windsor, Ontario. Being so exhausted, he fell asleep shortly after resting his head on the pillow.

"I'm not sure how long I was asleep," he says, "when I felt the sheets pull away from me and someone got into bed beside me. I could feel the weight. There was just no mistaking it. I think because I was so tired, I thought it was my wife. Then it hit me that it *couldn't be my wife because I wasn't at home and she certainly wasn't with me!* That's when I just sat bolt upright in bed and was suddenly wide awake. I turned the light on fast and there was, of course, no one there." His room number? *202.*

Another guest of this room I interviewed had a similar story with a twist. Monique had been reading in bed when she became tired, put her book on the bedside table, and turned off the light. She had been asleep for what she figures was half an hour when she was disturbed by the rustling of her bedsheets. She prefers to sleep with one or both of her feet outside of the blankets because she gets too hot. She heard the sheets rustling, then felt the blanket being pulled over her feet. She raised her head just a tad to see what was going on. The room was pitch dark so, of course, she couldn't see anything … that is until the light in the bathroom suddenly came on, illuminating a part of the bedroom. She shot up into a sitting position with the blankets tightly held around her. She timidly asked who was there. When she received no reply, she cautiously made her way out of bed, toward the bathroom. She was not surprised to find it empty. She wasn't sure what to do. She didn't want to call the front desk sounding like some hysterical woman with a crazy story. She tried to rationalize the event, thinking to herself that it was an old hotel and maybe the light switch was not fully depressed and had just popped up. She didn't really believe this but all seemed normal now, save for her slightly rattled nerves. She decided to retrieve her book and headed for a chair across the room. With the blanket still wrapped around her, she cuddled up in the chair for the night. Unlike others who managed to get back to sleep, she slept very little that night. Another difference was that she definitely believed in ghosts and felt that the room was haunted. She said a few words to the spirit, even thanking it for covering up her feet, but asked it if it would leave her alone for the rest of the night.

In another account, a guest named Diane was sleeping and was woken by a feeling that she was being nudged from the other side of the bed. She said that she actually fell out of the bed. When she got up, she came face to face with what she really believed was the ghost of a woman staring at her intensely. She said that the glare of those eyes was more jarring than being shoved out of bed. Unlike others, she requested another room for the night.

Another male guest recounts the story of feeling someone climbing into bed with him. He sat up and his eyes were drawn toward the hotel room door where he saw the figure of a young woman in a long white dress, like a ball gown or wedding dress. She was leaving the room. She glanced back at him, looking rather confused and sad. She then simply vanished through the closed door.

Staff members have reported that objects have flown off their cleaning carts while they were working in room 202. In one case, a staff member reported that after having changed the sheets and cleaning the bathroom, she returned to her cart to replace some incidentals in the room such as soap and shampoo. When she left the room, her cleaning cart had apparently left, too. She witnessed it making its merry way down the hallway by its own volition. She stood there for a second, not believing her eyes, and then ran after it. After catching up with it, she pulled it back to room 202, wanting to finish up this room immediately. When she entered the room with the intention of dropping off fresh towels, soap, and shampoo, she found that the bed she had just made was in complete disarray, as though someone had been tossing and turning in it all night. She quickly remade the bed and then not only left the room but the floor, requesting an early break.

The alleged story behind the haunting of room 202 is that a young couple named John and Mary had gotten married against the strenuous objections of the bride's father. They had in fact eloped. The father found out about this and beat the groom to death. Mary was so distraught that she took her own life. She is the supposed ghost of room 202. Another version of the legend reports that the new bride sent her husband out to purchase some medication she required but he was hit by a car and never returned to his new wife. Thus, she is seen wandering throughout the hotel in search of her beloved. Although one might wonder what urgent medication she was in need of that could not have been taken care of before her wedding night, the latter account would seem to ring most true. Although it may simply reflect on the author's research skills in the area of murders in old hotels, I have yet to uncover any record of the murder of a groom registered to room 202, and unless the perpetrator had some powerful connections, I would think that such an event would be a headline story. Still, I could be wrong and will continue to look.

Dinner For How Many?

In another case, an employee of the hotel who worked in the dining room spoke of seeing a gentleman seated at a table near a far window. He simply appeared to be looking out the window contemplatively. As the dining room was now closed, she approached the man to explain this to him. He turned to her and then … vanished. She ran away, not knowing what to except, wondering if she had perhaps lost her mind and, if so, hopefully only temporarily. It took her a few days before she would share this experience with anyone, including a co-worker who had also worked in the dining room and was quite sympathetic and understanding. In fact, her colleague even related some of the ghost stories that were associated with the hotel. This made her feel a tad better, but not by much. She had never believed in ghosts before, but she does now and she is not anxious to meet up with one again. I was curious about this because the apparition was not menacing toward her, so I wondered what she had been afraid of. I also inquired if she believed in any type of an afterlife. Her answer was very open and insightful and resonated the sentiment of many others I have spoken with. She related to me that she did believe in life after death but had become frightened because she was not prepared to come face to face with the "real thing." She asked, "Isn't there a saying about us fearing what we don't understand? Maybe if I saw one again, I might not react the same way. I might not be so afraid. And if it were in a haunted house; this was so unexpected. I do believe in life after death but I don't like to think we hang out in hotels or houses. I always believed we went on to a better place. I mean, I love working here and all but when I pass on, I don't want to stay here and be a ghost that someone else sees. It makes me wonder, why do they stay behind? And besides, I have my hands full with the live guests and the ghostly ones are not great tippers!" She concluded jokingly.

Still, other dining-room staff have reported carefully setting the table for the next mealtime, only to return a few minutes later to find plates and silverware displaced, and water goblets with napkins neatly folded and placed in the glasses turned upside down with the napkins on the floor or the plate.

The employee I quoted above had a good point and raised some poignant questions that have been posited by others in this book, with the prominent one being: Why do they stay behind? Although it may not apply to manifestations such as unsetting tables or the unmaking of beds, there are theories being explored. The two most widely held are that what people are actually witnessing is not the actual spirit of the deceased but the residual energy of their previous presence. In physics, all things are energy vibrating at different frequencies. As parapsychologist Andrew Nichols, PhD, states: "We generate electromagnetic fields by our thought processes and biological activity … many of these so-called [haunted houses] are constructed of materials that would be easily be magnetized such as brick, which, for example, contains saline and silica, the same thing you find in recording tape. These imprints are scanned directly into the physical structure [of the environment] and a person's brain that is especially sensitive to these fields … it's possible that their brain could act as a VCR and decode this recorded material."

In physics, nothing ever "goes away," but when certain conditions converge, it can "turn on" or charge this residual energy. As just stated, one can think of it as watching a video that was set to play by a combination of environmental factors including electrical storms.

That may be why many ghost stories share the popular theme of a dark and *stormy* night where the air is charged with negative ions. Other elements may trigger the manifestation, as well. Sometimes it is a simple matter of a sensitive or psychic individual entering the room who either acts as a conduit for the stored energy or as a person who has the psychic ability known as *retrocognition.* Retrocognition is the ability to tune into or become aware of events that occurred at a given place and time that the perceiver would not have normal, practical, or explainable way of knowing.

Either way, the effect is that the events that have been imprinted or "recorded" in cases of residual manifestations are in a type of feedback loop that can be activated or turned on by many variable factors.

The other theory is that the actual spirit or *essence* of the deceased individual may have either become trapped in a tragic event and is "reliving" it over and over again. This is often a distressing notion to people, as the soul would seem to be locked in a kind of purgatory. On the other hand, they may be trying to let their story be known, which is still a tragic entrapment. Oftentimes, once the true circumstances of the event have been revealed it is often enough to set the spirit free. In cases where this does not happen and the spirit simply cannot seem to let go of it and move on, psychics such as Madeline employ techniques that help the spirit *to let go and move on* (providing they want to). On the surface, this is not all that difficult to understand when we consider some of the things that happen to us in life that we have great difficulty in getting over and moving on. We, too, live it over and over again in our minds. We have a sense of the absence of justice and closure, so we are left with unfinished business. This is not restricted to things that are done to us, but sometimes things that happen to us, such as accidents. This may be the case with the haunted elevator in the Fort Garry Hotel.

A former guest of the hotel (in fact, she has stayed at this hotel on numerous occasions), entered a particular elevator and noticed a young man with a tool box standing at the back. He simply stared straight ahead, not even giving her a nod or a glance. She did not look back even once, but felt a strong sense that she was being stared at. She stated that she felt a cold chill on her back. She was relieved when the elevator stopped, admitting one gentleman. She and the man smiled and said hello, but she noted that the two men made no such salutations. When she reached her floor a few seconds later, she turned to nod a good day to the gentleman and was shocked to see that the young man with the tool box was not in the elevator. He certainly had not left by any conventional means.

The apparition she most likely encountered was one Mr. Rutherford. He was a maintenance man. He began working for the hotel in 1911, two years before its official opening; other work in construction and installation were also underway. Mr. Rutherford was called upon to inspect what was then the main elevator, which was losing its counterbalance. Something went terribly wrong and the elevator gave way, plummeting the poor man to his death. This guest is not the only witness to this doomed repairman. Hopefully he is not doomed but this is an example of an event replaying itself when the right trigger presents itself. There are also numerous accounts of the elevator malfunctioning in minor ways: lights flickering, the air ventilation shutting off, stopping on a floor that was not requested by anyone on the elevator. Sometimes these malfunctions caused an inspection of the elevator, only to reveal a mechanical problem that would have gone undetected if these minor malfunctions had not drawn the attention of the inspector. Perhaps Mr. Rutherford is still on the job!

Whatever the cause of these inexplicable events, it is such a lovely hotel and anyone staying at the Fort Gerry Hotel is sure to have a pleasant, "spirited" time. Just do not expect to receive a discount for sharing your room if you happen to have found yourself booked into room 202! Also, be rest assured that the elevator is being well looked after.

A Political Ghost of a Chance: Part II

This portion of the chapter began with the experiences of a politician who by chance found herself in a purportedly haunted hotel; however, she is by no means the first politician to have a brush with the paranormal. In some cases, it was not a mere "brush." Some actively sought it out while others would appear to be the instigators of the manifestations. Such is the case with William Lyon Mackenzie, Toronto's first mayor and leader of the failed government rebellion of 1837 in the province of Ontario (then known as Upper Canada). Mackenzie was a fine, honest man who abhorred corruption of any kind, especially in government. Although his intentions were honourable, the failed rebellion forced him into political exile in the United States. It was either that or face imprisonment or even the gallows, which was the fate that almost befell one of his greatest supporters, John Montgomery. The judgment was commuted and Mr. Montgomery lived to reach nearly one hundred years old (not bad for a man sentenced to death by hanging).

Perhaps coincidently, he cursed those he accused of offering perjured testimony against him during his trail. Two of those men later committed suicide. If they were guilty, I suspect their deaths were more a matter of conscience than curses, but who knows. Whatever the case, after receiving a pardon and upon returning to Canada, Mackenzie managed with great difficulty to secure for himself and his family a home at 82 Bond Street. The house remains there still, designated as a historical monument. It's apparently much more than that, however. Stories began to surface about the strange occurrences taking place within the house after a couple who had been former caretakers made public statements to a now-defunct newspaper. The name of the couple was the Edmunds. The stories were taken quite seriously since the Edmunds were a respectable, sober couple who certainly had nothing to gain by going public with their story. In fact, the majority of people keep such experiences to themselves for fear of being called crazy, amongst other things. Newspapers do not generally publish such stories in order to maintain their reputation as a serious source of legitimate news. The exception is, of course, Halloween, when such stories will pop up in the special interest section of the paper.

Further, the stories that all the family members related were consistent and in no way contradictory. Although the Edmunds knew nothing of the Mackenzie family including William Lyon himself, the former resident of the house, the Edmunds reported seeing the figure of "a little bald man in a frock coat." That fit the description of the former resident, but what is interesting here is that although Mr. Mackenzie was indeed bald, this was not common knowledge since he always wore a hairpiece when he was in public. In fact there were not even any pictures of him sans hairpiece, and being such a well known and at times controversial public figure, there were a great deal of photographs taken of him. On one occasion, the grandchildren had been staying over. They were on the third floor and had to visit the bathroom during the night, which was located on the second floor. Shortly after entering the bathroom, their grandparents were awakened by the terrified screams of the little ones who claim to have seen the ghostly image of a woman who simply vanished before their eyes. The Edmunds also experienced what is pretty much standard fare for ghostly manifestations. They reported hearing footsteps on the stairs, toilets flushing, music emanating from an unoccupied room, the distinct sounds of the old-style printing press running, and ghostly voices. The two manifestations that do not really hold up is the sound of the printing press. The printing press that would have been used by Mr. Mackenzie; it had a characteristic sound to it that did not match the sound that the Edmunds described. As such printing presses had long since been obsolete, it is understandable that the Edmunds would not be able to differentiate between the sounds of the old-style printing presses with the newer ones. Nevertheless, the fact that they heard the sound of a printing press at all remains poignant in that they had no knowledge of there having ever been a printing press in the residence at all. The other manifestation that doesn't hold up is the sound of the flushing toilet. It is probably unrelated to the actual Mackenzie family because at the time the Mackenzie family actually lived in the house, there were no flush toilets.

The most outstanding manifestation in this haunting in that it is *very rare* happened to Mrs. Edmunds. One evening in the year 1958, Mrs. Edmunds was awoken from a sound sleep. Above her hovered a ghostly image that she had in fact seen before, only this time it was right above her. A short period of time transpired before the apparition suddenly slapped Mrs. Edmunds across the face! After Mr. Edmunds had convinced his rather upset wife that she had only had a nightmare, she managed to go back to sleep. However, the following morning, when she looked in the mirror, she saw a red bruise on the cheek that had been slapped. She assumed the assault had been delivered by the same woman she had seen on another occasion. Mrs. Edmonds was quite frightened by the sight of this woman. Her first encounter with her was not quite so traumatic.

Mrs. Edmunds had been asleep when she was woken up by a touch on her shoulder. She looked up to see what was an almost solid figure of this woman, who was so close to her that her long brown hair nearly dangled on her pillow. Then she simply vanished. (There was also another woman who also had long hair, wore an old-fashioned dress, and seemed to wander the halls aimlessly. This could be the same woman that the children saw.) Who this woman was or what the purpose of this assault was is completely unknown and hard to fathom. As earlier stated, such a violent, physical assault from any ghostly manifestation is extremely rare, although it is more common in cases involving poltergeists (the latter, which, by the author's estimation, is unrelated to actual ghosts). Most injuries incurred by people encountering ghosts are as a result of their own panicked reaction, such as fleeing down a flight of stairs in such haste that they trip and fall.

The officials in charge of the Mackenzie House staunchly deny any ghostly happenings; however, that being the case, one cannot wonder why they secured the services of an Anglican priest to bless the house. Unfortunately or fortunately, depending on your point of view, the blessing was not entirely successful since reports of the haunting continued, though they have since died down substantially. Perhaps William Lyon Mackenzie has finally moved on. This is not the end of the Mackenzie story, though. William Lyon Mackenzie had a grandson, William Lyon Mackenzie King, who was Canada's longest-serving prime minister. Politics was not the only thing that ran in the family, however. The Prime Minister had a great interest in the "supernatural" and in making contact with the other side. He reportedly began regular seances from 1932 to 1935. He was not prime minister during this time. He pursued his contact with the dead, or as they referred to it, "reaching beyond the veil" along with his longtime friend and confidante, Joan Patteson.

These seances were conducted on a regular and frequent basis in King's home, the famous Laurier House so named after yet another former prime minister, Wilfred Laurier. Their instrument of communication was a simple table ("table rapping" was a very common way of connecting with the dead in those days, especially in England, Canada, and the United States). King and Patteson had their own method and code worked out, which varied from the common form of table rapping whereby knocks would be heard directly from the table, often something simple like one rap for no, two for yes, three for perhaps, etc. In the King and Patteson sessions, they had an actual leg of the table rapping and its raps would correspond with letters of the alphabet. For instance, one tap represented the letter A, two taps the letter B, etc. This must have been very time-consuming, but their patience apparently paid off as they reportedly made contact with a number of historical figures and, more importantly to King, he established contact with his much-loved, deceased mother from whom, as in life, he sought frequent counsel.

The psychic activity did not end with the passing of William Lyon Mackenzie King. Laurier House, which is now a public museum, is perhaps not surprisingly reported to be haunted. While he was still alive, King arranged his third-floor study in such a way as to be a monument to his mother. (In fact, the entire residence has been restored to appear as it did when Mackenzie lived there, but the third-floor study is of special significance due to the connection with his mother.) While he was alive, King always left a lamp on near this very important room. In order to recreate and enhance the historical ambience, a lamp was left on when tourists visited the house. Turning the lamp off was a whole other matter. When the house was locked up for the night, a security person would turn the light off. No sooner would they step way from it, sometimes making it all the way down to the second floor, when they would hear the distinct sound of the light being turned back on. Upon investigating the source of the sound, the light would be found to be shining brightly!

This event would repeat itself over and over again. The security guard would finally give up and leave the light on. To ensure that these events were not due to a faulty switch, which could be a potential fire hazard, the light was inspected but nothing was found to be wrong with it. Some things you just have to learn how to live with. Although impressions, no matter how intense they may be, are not empirical evidence of paranormal activity, many people who visited the house swore they would never do so again because they felt the presence of unseen persons. They had no doubt in their minds that the house was most certainly haunted.

In one case, a woman and her husband visiting from British Columbia, witnessed the aforementioned light in the third-floor study growing slowly brighter until it reached a point were it hurt their eyes to look at it. Consequently, they turned their heads away and when they turned back to face the lamp, it was emitting the normal degree of light for the bulb's wattage. At the same time, they reported feeling a cool breeze pass by them as though someone had just opened a window. These experiences have been reported by others, as well. Some have also reported that upon leaving the study, they stopped dead in their tracks and looked back into the study because they heard what they thought were voices conversing. Some people felt such strong impressions from the house, or even had some of these experiences, that they refused to accept employment in the museum no matter how badly they might be in need of a job. It is important to note that being a tourist destination, people from all over Canada and even parts of Europe would visit this historic site and not all of them (in fact many Canadians) were not aware of these ghostly stories. King's influence apparently extended beyond the Mackenzie house to his vacation property in Quebec. He had also conducted seances there. Since his demise, there have been numerous eyewitness reports of seeing the actual image of William Lyon Mackenzie King.

Just on a side note, King's activities were known amongst his fellow members of parliament, as well as close friends and the public in general. However, the times were very different back then. Nothing is sacrosanct these days; privacy barely exists with almost anything being fuel for the fodder. If he were in office in this time and age, instead of being the longest-running prime minister in office, the House of Commons would have made Canadian back bacon out of him back when he was leader of the opposition! Thankfully, this man and his grandfather left us a great legacy and are forever a colourful part of our Canadian history and heritage.

A Gothic Tale of City Hall

Watercolourist, William Armstrong

Painted rendition of Old City Hall, Toronto, Ontario.

In the city of Toronto, Ontario, there stands a large, red sandstone building that was erected in 1898. It is quite an impressive and rather imposing structure. It was designed by Toronto architect Edward James Lennox (who also designed the magnificent Casa Loma in Toronto). Amongst many of its striking features is a bevy of gargoyles, a 260-foot clock tower, and a grand marble staircase. Understandably, it could be mistaken for part of a set from a gothic mystery movie. Its original function was the housing of the offices for the municipal government for the city of Toronto. For the past few decades it has been used as courthouses. Not surprisingly, this marvellous old gothic structure also comes complete with ghosts. It is thought that at least two trapped spirits are those of Arthur Lucas and Ron Turpin, the last two men to be hanged in Canada before the abolishment of the death penalty in 1976. Arthur Lucas was an American convicted of killing a drug-dealing FBI informant and Ron Turpin was convicted of inflicting a fatal gunshot wound to a police officer. They were sentenced to death on December 11, 1962. At 2:02 a.m. they were hanged back to back at the "Old" Don Jail (another haunted and daunting structure that that has been sealed since 1993, but that's another story). They died together. The sentencing took place in courtroom 33, probably the most haunted place in the courthouse. One janitor tells the story of his encounter with one of the phantoms of courtroom 33. He was mopping the floor when he suddenly became aware of a presence in the room. He looked up and clearly saw the figure of a wretched-looking man, unshaven and stony-faced with anger and determination. He did not seem to take any notice of the janitor and stared straight ahead. He remained suspended for a few seconds and then was suddenly propelled forward, coming straight for the janitor. He was gliding effortlessly through the air, his feet a few inches from the floor. He passed straight through the janitor, causing the poor man to feel a chill and a slight breeze.

As with some of the cleaning staff mentioned previously in this chapter, there are staff employed in this facility who outright refuse to work in certain rooms. Considering this man's experience, who can blame them?

Night watchmen are also witnesses to paranormal activity. One spoke of repeatedly hearing footsteps and other noises such as doors slamming, knocks against doors and walls, and clanging against metal filing cabinets. Another heard the sound of the judge's gavel coming down. Being a night watchman, you can appreciate how much more difficult their jobs were made as they were of course obliged to investigate any unusual activity. That explains why they tended to respond more with frustration and irritation to these events as opposed to fear. More so, they were alone in a building that was supposed to be empty of living persons.

On one evening, a watchman was doing his rounds, dutifully checking that the lights were out and the doors were locked. Upon completing this task, he headed for the exit from the second floor when he heard the squeaking sounds of doors slowly swaying. He directed his flashlight down the length of the corridor and noticed that three of the doors that had just been locked were now partially open. One of the doors was to courtroom 33 … and the lights were on. Most of the investigations turned up nothing, but there were occasions when upon entering a room from which there had been a disturbance, some things were discovered to be amiss. For instance, law books would be on the floor or a window would be open. On one occasion, a large oak table at which lawyers would be seated when court proceedings were in session, had been shoved toward the judges' bench. These tables are enormously heavy, requiring a great deal of manpower to move half an inch, let alone several metres!

There are still other witnesses to these events. If there is truth to the adage about being sober as a judge, then a couple of witnesses are quite reliable sources since they are judges. They spoke of hearing footsteps in the stairwell, either ahead or behind them, but when they looked ahead or behind, there was not a soul in sight. One judge also stated that on more than one occasion, he felt a tug on his robes (one judge even went public with this experience, quite an unusual move for a person in such a position and profession). On different occasions, some of the judges would be working late and, except for the night watchmen, should have been alone in the building yet they would hear footsteps, doors opening and closing, as well as toilets flushing. The back stairwell that the staff had used that was mentioned above is another hot spot. As mentioned before, one judge felt his robes being tugged at. Others would hear steps following them up the stairs and when they stopped, the footsteps following them would also cease. Upon moving again, the phantom footsteps would also resume. One judge even reported receiving a shove, fortunately from behind — if it had been from the front, he may have toppled backward, possibly receiving an injury. Still, whenever the footsteps were heard trailing behind them, they would turn around asking, "Who's there?" and receive no reply. Yet another judge, upon entering his office, discovered that several of his books were piled up on a filing cabinet and the chair that was suppose to be at his desk was instead against a wall directly facing his desk. At the time of writing of this, none of the staff is aware of any further anomalous activity, or at least nothing they are willing to admit to or discuss.

But I'm Still Here: Beyond and Back Again

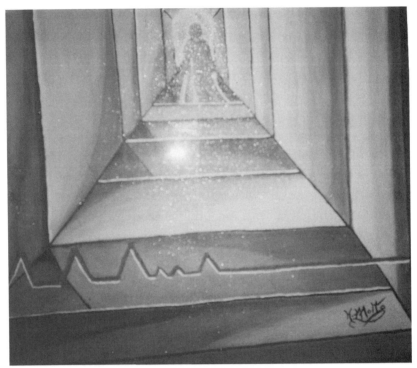

Author's rendition of near death experience.

Michelle Willson is now a forty-eight-year-old nurse living in Hounslow, England. However, when this death experience took place (I say "death" as opposed to "near death" because she was actually dead, not near death) she was only eleven years old. She was in for a tonsillectomy and in those days a patient would be put under general anaesthetic. Young Michelle did not respond well to the anaesthesia and in fact had a fatal reaction to it. They worked tirelessly in an attempt to revive her before pronouncing her dead. The staff was in shock and dismay. The following is an account in her own words.

"I saw the surgeon rip off his gloves and toss them in frustration and disgust. The anaesthesiologist leaned dejectedly over his equipment, shaking his head. One of the nurses was quietly sobbing. Meanwhile, I was above all of this, wondering what the fuss was all about. They were acting as though someone had just died or something. Then I looked at the body on the operating table and realized *it was me!* I was astonished. I tried to cry out to them, 'Hey you guys! It's all right. I'm right here! Can't you hear me? Can't you see me?' But of course they couldn't see the *real me.* They could only see the body. I tried so hard to make myself heard and my presence felt. It was the must frustrating experience I have ever had in my life! Then I heard a voice off in the distance calling my name. I turned toward it and there was a beautiful being of light. I thought it was an angel. There appeared to be wings and a flowing robe but it was all light. I started to make my way toward this angelic being that just radiated pure light and love but a force from her held me back. Otherwise, I would have readily gone. Without actually speaking, she made these words very clear to me: 'Michelle, it is not your time. You must go back.' And with that, I felt pushed, almost forced back into that lifeless form. I hated it. It was like falling from a great height and it really hurt. The OR came to life with the sound of 'beep, beep, beep.' Everybody started scrambling like crazy. Apparently I wasn't out of the woods yet because I could still see what was going on. The surgeon was barking, 'Bring her up! Bring her up!' They finally got me stabilized but I was still on all the vital sign monitors and was not yet able to breathe on my own.

"I was moved into the ICU recovery. There was one nurse in particular ... her name was Illene ... she was new to the ward and was very frightened or nervous. She said to the charge nurse who was about to go on her break, 'You're not going to leave me alone with her, are you?' The charge nurse assured her that I would be all right and if anything did happen, she (the nurse) would not be on her own. I, too, was trying to assure her that I was all right, I was right here. Eventually, to everyone's relief, I came around and that was that; at least for them. It will never be over for me. That experience changed me forever. I will never be the same. I don't look at life or death the same way as most people and from that young age on, when most children don't think about such things, I contemplated matters of life, death, and the afterlife seriously. I use to ask questions but it seemed to frighten my parents and put people off so I just read a lot of books and kept my thoughts and questions to myself. It was that experience that caused me from an early age to become a nurse. In that, I was quite committed."

The Present

"The next incident that happened to me took place over twenty years later. I had never been particularly close my mother. We had a turbulent relationship but she was my mother and I loved her. In the summer of 2005, she was diagnosed with ovarian cancer. There was no chance. It had been caught too late and was in an advanced state. By the end of November, the end was drawing near. By this time I had been in nursing for many years, so I took a leave of absence from work to take personal care of her. Her major concern was that the family have a happy Christmas, not a mournful one. She had me running around fulfilling specific, carefully detailed and constructed plans for the holiday, from the dinner to the presents she wanted me to purchase for my siblings and the grandchildren. I obliged her, showing her each gift I had purchased to ensure they met her specifications. The last gift was for my brother and his wife. It wasn't quite right, so I exchanged it and she was satisfied with that new one. With all the preparations taken care of, right down to what type of Christmas tree we would have and where it would be, she passed peacefully away.

"The family tried their best to make this a happy celebration, not only for the sake of the grandchildren, but also as a celebration of our mother's life and in honour of her dying wish that we celebrate Christmas, not hold a wake.

"Christmas morning (not *mourning*) finally arrived. All the carefully chosen presents were distributed, all tagged 'With love from Mom.' My siblings fought back tears as they opened these carefully chosen gifts but they also opened them with a smile and great care. The children simply tore into theirs with glee, of course. When we were done with the presents, my eight-year-old niece pointed out that there was still one more little present nestled right in the tree. I was confused by this, as I had not placed any presents in the tree. My niece removed it from the tree and, reading the label, handed it over, saying it was for me. Now I was really confused. All eyes were on me. I had purchased all the other presents as instructed but I certainly had not bought one for myself. I looked at my siblings and they just stared blankly at me, as confused as I was. None of them had purchased it and the presents they had bought me were certainly not tagged 'With love from Mom.' I unwrapped it. Inside was a small jewelry box. Upon opening it, I not only gasped, but almost dropped it. My sister-in-law came rushing forward as if to steady me, and my brother asked with some concern what it was. The box contained a heart-shaped locket imbedded with a single pearl. On the back was an inscription from the book of Psalms, *The Lord is my Shepherd*, and when I opened the locket, on the right side was a picture of me and on the left was a smiling picture of my mother. If all this were not enough, the thing about this locket is that I received an identical one on the occasion of my confirmation almost thirty years before. I cherished it. In fact, it was the first real 'grown-up' piece of jewelry I had ever received. When we moved from Guilford to Hounslow, I had lost it. I was heartbroken! For years, and I mean *years*, I looked for another locket like it, to no avail. It was and is unique. My siblings had long since forgotten about it and never understood why I was making such a fuss about it in the first place, so even if they wanted to give me a special, sentimental gift, it would not have been that particular piece of jewelry. And now, after all these years, here it was in my hands again. I immediately placed it around my neck and have not taken it off since and never will until the day I die. At that time, I intend to pass it down to my daughter. One other thing about the locket; everything about it was identical to the one I received for my confirmation except for one thing. The one I 'originally' had contained a picture of me on the right side and Mother Mary on the left. This one had a picture of my mother in place of Mother Mary. Although we had had a strained relationship, I felt at peace with her now and that for the first time in my life, I had a real Mom. *Thank you, Mom, and Merry Christmas.*"

[Author's note: On a personal note, which I am always reluctant to engage in, these stories came to me at a very poignant time. I was at a point when I did not know if there was even going to be a second book in me to finish. Just prior to receiving Michelle's remarkable stories, I had just learned of the impending death of my own mother. The timing was uncanny, to say the least. Like Michelle, I, too, had had a strained relationship with my mother. At first my mother seemed to be at peace with the news, almost happy-go-lucky. I knew this would not last for long. Sure enough, on Thursday the seventh of September, when I spoke to her, she was quite despondent. I was upset for her. I myself had been quite depressed all along, not just by this news but also because this would be the third death in my family in the past two years. I would be alone, in regards to immediate family anyway. I was at the end of my ropes and felt totally spent. That night, I retired to bed at the usual time. I was not ill so my fiancé had not stayed over that night. Just after 12:00 a.m., I was suddenly awoken by a presence in the room. In my sleepy state, I thought it was my boyfriend. I had been sleeping facing the window so I turned to face the door and began to ask who I thought was my fiancé what was wrong, but stopped in midsentence. It was not my fiancé at all. I was face to face with the figure of the hooded monk I had first encountered in our family home on Merion Street in the 1970s. Although the room had been cool, it was now warm and comfortable. There was no mistaking the power and presence of this entity. (To this day, he is still being seen on that street, as is documented in Chapter 1 of this book.) I was mesmerized and for some crazy reason, the only thought that entered my mind was, "Hello, old friend. Long time no see." He communicated to me in no uncertain terms that "You are charged with a mission that must be completed. Remember!" As I began to rise, he vanished. Although he did not speak the words, by mission, I knew he was referring to this second manuscript, which I felt had withered and died in me like an unborn child. It had been buried with all those loved ones I had lost. I interpreted "remember" to mean the message I had received from him, what two of the consulting psychics on my books had said had been from the Monk: "Death does not possess you. You possess death and acquire its magic." We took magic to mean transforming power and wisdom and that much

of life is an illusion. I also remembered the message we had received from the sitting, which I had thought was directed at someone else about not being able to turn back (AREEL, Chapter 1). Although I have never fully grasped the deeper meaning or intent of the first message, I was certainly traversing the valley of the shadow of death. In fact, I was practically on a first-name basis with the Grim Reaper. The following day, I felt strangely imbued by the timely visit of this enigmatic entity but still felt trapped like a caged animal. I had been sickened, at times paralyzed, by the onslaught of overwhelming, negative events. How could I possibly make contact with the book buried within me? How could I even begin writing again? Nevertheless, I felt heavily burdened by this "charge" that was upon me. Later on that day, I received the most amazing phone call. One of the aforementioned psychics in England (Julian) had put a woman in touch with me. She had been emailing me but I had been too ill to get out and retrieve my messages. That very day, being Friday the eighth, she felt an overwhelming urge to phone me directly. She was calling all the way from Hounslow, England. "Coincidently," Hounslow is the name of my publisher, owned by the Dundurn Group. She had two stories to share with me and was anxious that they be published since she passionately believed that they would be of comfort and benefit to others (her compulsion and belief was so strong that she invested a good deal of time and money carefully relating the stories to me). Little did she know that she had already accomplished that for at least one person; she knew nothing of my circumstances. The stories she related to me are the ones presented above. She lit a spark in me, which enabled me to begin writing again. I promised her that I would write up the accounts immediately and e-mail them to her for her perusal. I always keep my word so write it up I did. Her stories could not have come at a better time. It was no mere coincidence. It afforded me the means to address the situation I was facing with my own mother and reminded me that there is no real death, just change, as drastic and painful as that change may be. I am sure it will do the same for others who read it, as well. And it forced and inspired me to start writing again, to take up the "charge" as it were. All this from a hooded monk from long past and a "stranger" from Hounslow.

Thank you, Michelle from Hounslow, and again, hello old friend returned from maybe a better time and place. I guess I have accepted "my charge." So once again, I find myself standing on the shores of the river Rubicon. God help me or at least toss me the occasional life preserver. We can all use one of those at times.]

NO PARKING
BURIAL ZONE

You living people, you understand so little about us. As you stray through the world's shadows, spare a thought now and then for those on the other side. Every time you think of us or pray for us, a firework will burst in the heavens, and the light it creates will shower down upon you, will help you and enlighten you.

In the year 1827, the founder of the city of Guelph, Ontario, John Galt, established its first cemetery, known simply as the Public Burying Ground. That place is now the Baker Street Parking Lot (places an odd

Photo by Kimberly Molto

Picture of Baker Street Parking Lot.

twist on an old song, "they tore down the trees and put in a parking lot," only in this case, they dug up the graves and put in a parking lot.)

Legislation was passed that no more bodies were to be buried within the fast-growing city limits. The remains were moved to the Woodlawn Cemetery (then known as Union Cemetery, *circa* 1854) as well as to some other cemeteries. Ninety-eight bodies in all were re-interred at that time.

Fast forward to October 13, 2005. A sinkhole had developed near the entrance of the Baker Street Parking Lot. (It is not unusual that a graveyard would be situated here as there are three churches directly beside the parking lot — before it was a parking lot.) A work crew was deployed to repair the damage. During the repairs, at approximately 4:11 p.m., much to the shock and confusion of one of the workmen, the skeletal remains of what appeared to be a human were discovered. Naturally, work was suspended immediately and the police and coroner were contacted. On October 14, the bones were carefully removed to the Guelph Police Station where it was subsequently determined by the coroner that the remains were indeed human. All in all, the bodies of two women and a man, in addition to fifteen other bodies, have been uncovered over time. All the bodies are re-interred at the newly opened section of Woodlawn Cemetery, officially known as Woodlawn Memorial Park. When the parking lot was first built and the bodies moved, the identity of the deceased was not known as record-keeping was not very good in past times. Thus, many of the bodies are scattered about through Woodlawn, some in unmarked graves, again, because the identities were simply unknown. However, with the opening of the new addition to Woodlawn, a monument has been erected in honour and memory of all those re-interred; it is also a reminder of Guelph's past and the pioneers who worked so hard to build the city. Meanwhile, as work continues on the Baker Street Parking Lot (and as more bodies may be uncovered, particularly behind what was once the post office adjacent to the parking lot) the monument stands ready to receive them. To quote from an old episode of the *Twilight Zone*, "*Room for one more ...*"

Photo by Kimberly Molto

Monument in dedication of the pioneers whose remains were reburied at Woodlawn Memorial.

The story does not end or even begin here, however. Over the years there have been several reports of sightings and other oddities. Not much was made of it because being a parking lot, people are coming and going and car alarms are going off easily. However, there are some incidents that cannot be so easily dismissed. One such occasion took place around 5:00 p.m. on a Thursday. A car park attendant noticed a woman dressed in what he referred to as "turn of the century" clothing; a long skirt and a bonnet-type hat. She was wandering around the parking lot, not as though she were looking for her car, but in fact she seemed quite confused by the presence of all the automobiles (he wants to stress that this was only his impression, but she was genuinely lost). She seemed out of place and "out of this world." Indeed, she could have most certainly been out of this world and not looking for her car but instead for her relocated grave. He thought to himself that (at that time), the parking lot was not all that far from the Guelph Little Theatre so perhaps she was coming from a dress rehearsal, though he did not really believe this. He further speculated that she was ill or on

170

drugs but she was not staggering or anything; just wandering about, lost and confused. He observed her for a while and was going to leave the toll booth to see if he could assist her when two cars in succession came up to the window of the booth. When he looked for her, she was nowhere to be found. This is not the only individual who has seen this mysterious lady. One patron, upon getting into her car, caught sight of the mystery lady and was so mesmerized that she did not fully get into her car but stood halfway up watching this woman wander about. The patron described the same style of dress and apparent state of confusion as did the car park attendant. This patron was a regular at the Baker Street Parking Lot because she attended a church adjacent to the lot. There have been other reports of a man in his late thirties with a beard and hat wandering about. Again, he has been described as wearing turn-of-the-century garb. People don't really make much of it because these apparitions look quite real, certainly not like "traditional" ghostly figures, but as I have stressed in both my books and lectures, apparitions do not necessarily look like something out of a Dickens novel or Stephen King, either. (Thank God for that!) That being said, some of them do. (I was once asked, How would you know if your house was haunted or not? I answered by reversing the question: How could you not know? Say you have dinner guests over and while everyone is peacefully seated around the table, the candles, which were not lit, suddenly ignite. The lights that were on a dimmer suddenly hit the room as though floodlights were turned on and the temperature takes a sudden nosedive. What would you think, especially when such anomalous events repeat themselves?)

But I digress ... back to Baker Street. On more than one occasion, the lights in the parking lot have for no explainable reason grown remarkably bright, with some blowing out. One car park attendant looked up from his paper, preparing himself to attend to a car, which he heard coming and saw two lights, but when he put his paper down and looked in the direction of the supposedly oncoming vehicle, there was nothing there. On other occasions, children have been heard laughing as though playing in the parking lot, which of course is not allowed. Yet upon investigation, no children could be found. Many people have told me they feel very uncomfortable walking toward their cars and can't wait to get safely in their vehicles and get out of the parking lot. They often feel as though they are not alone and being watched or followed, yet there is no one in sight. These things happen to men and women during the day and night.

Unfortunately, hauntings of this nature are somewhat ambiguous and primarily based on personal accounts, thus rendering them difficult, if not impossible, to investigate or verify. However, the fact that so many people saw the same images without having communicated with each other, and given that most of these individuals were not aware that this was once the site of a former graveyard, it does lend some impressive credence to the reports.

This now brings us back to Woodlawn Cemetery. In December of 2005, the author; a technician, Ian Godfrey; one of the lead psychics for the book, Madeline Kinney; and a telepath, Chris Howard, were all gathered in the cemetery for an evening event of which we discretely departed from. We gingerly made our way through parts of the cemetery to see if we could pick anything up. It was quite relaxed and casual, though we were freezing our toes off. Fortunately, the cold had no effect on the infrared camera or tape recorder. As we were strolling and chatting, we all suddenly stopped short. We smelled ozone and it felt like we had walked into a wall of ice. We even put our hands in the cold spot and withdrew them to verify the temperature change as others have done when they felt cold spots. There was no doubt about it; this was a genuine, localized cold spot. Without even thinking, Ian began shooting and hit the record button. Madeline received the impression of a woman in a long skirt and bonnet. Chris heard a woman say the name "Molly." We were not at any gravesite, in fact we were in between trees (some of the original gravesites are unmarked and the location of many of them are unknown). We all felt the distinct presence of a woman, though. Later, when we checked the film, the very location where we felt the presence and the cold spot on the film was a very clear picture of a solid, "ethereal" mist. After nearly two minutes of white noise, over the tape recorder came the sound of a sigh and we could barely make out the name Molly. Upon computer enhancement, it became clearer. There was definitely a sigh and weak voice there. Could this be the woman that was seen wandering through the Baker Street Parking Lot? The description fit and neither Chris nor Madeline knew of the story or description of the woman seen wandering the lot. Perhaps she had finally found her new resting place.

Victorian Valhalla: City of the Dead

As with the story of the crash of Flight 401, another story that has fascinated me since the 1970s was that of the so-called Highgate Vampire (no, this is not a story about so-called vampires, which is more in the category of Bigfoot and UFOs/aliens, which has nothing to do with parapsychology). Nevertheless, the story of a vampire haunting the cemetery made international news, so was my first introduction to Highgate Cemetery, often referred to as the Victorian Valhalla (in Nordic mythology, Valhalla was the hall of the dead), which opened in 1839, at the same time as a municipal cholera outbreak. At the time, it was a very posh place with long Victorian funeral processions attended by the very wealthy dressed in their finest black. It must have been quite a sight to behold. Years later, I would have the pleasure of making the acquaintance of a couple, Rodger and Wanda Taylor, who live in a very large Victorian house overlooking a part of this extremely large cemetery. In fact it is so large (over 37 acres, two of which are on "unconsecrated" ground, which would be ideal for vampires I suppose) the word "cemetery" is inaccurate; the correct word would be "necropolis" (i.e. city of the dead) and this "city" is home to over 165,000 people or, more politically correct, the living impaired. Amongst some of its most notable residents are Karl Marx and the nineteenth-century physicist Michael Faraday (of the famed Faraday cage that I have written about in this book). Even if you are not one who includes visiting cemeteries amongst your "must see" places while on vacation, should you ever find yourself in London, England, this is an amazing place to see or, rather, experience.

The necropolis is divided into two sections. The newer is the East section, where you will find Karl Marx, and the older, now restricted-access West section. This is this section that Rodger and Wanda's house overlooks. Unlike the East section, the West section is not open to the public except through booked tours only. I received a good feel of the west side while travelling up Swain's Lane, a very steep road that runs alongside the west part of the necropolis, to visit Rodger and Wanda. One of the first things that took my breath away were locked ornate and imposing gates that were the entrance to the closed west end. The stories about strange sightings and sounds by people traversing this road date back to before the 1960s and many came from people passing by this ominous north gate along Swain's Lane. I do not wonder at this, as the place is ripe for such stories. It's a horror/ghost movie waiting to happen. In fact, it has been the setting for more than one horror film and purportedly was the inspiration for one particular scene in Bram Stoker's *Dracula*. The scene is one that involves a family's subterranean burial chamber, and to this day, people swear they hear voices emanating from the chamber, even though it's been bricked over for many years now. As happens with many older cemeteries, as the years passed by, both sides of the necropolis fell to neglect until 1975 when a group calling themselves "The Friends of Highgate" took charge of affairs, cleaning things up, restoring what tombstones they could, and restricted access, which has been successful in curtailing the vandalism and other unwelcome visitors (I refer to some groups of people who felt this was the ideal place to engage in certain "occult" and satanic rituals, which, needless to say, sullied the graveyard's reputation and dignity).

Upon entering the necropolis, one cannot help but feel that they have been transported back in time. You certainly do not feel you are within the boundaries of the thriving metropolis of London, England, especially because it was so unnaturally quiet. Although the east side has been cleaned and restored as much as possible, the west side is another story. There you will find overgrowths of vines, ivy, and moss covering tombstones and paths leading into a somewhat foreboding forest. In fact, there are many such paths and I couldn't help but think of the Black Forest, even though I have never seen it. Passing through the north gates you feel as though you are about to enter another world.

The gates themselves seem to give off the sense of being told HALT! One is greeted with numerous bushes, vegetation, ivy, and trees where small headstones, broken columns, crosses, and torches project through. Every now and then, you would catch a glimpse of an angel or a headstone jutting out here and there.

Photo courtesy of Rodger Taylor

The spooky, unkempt side of Highgate Cemetery.

Passing through an archway are two foreboding, large columns. This was the entrance to what is called Egyptian Avenue; on the opposite side of the circle is St. Michael's Church, where Wanda was to do her photo shoot. Here, there is a row of continuous family vaults that form a pathway to the Circle of Lebanon. (Something I found fascinating and made special note of were the myriad funeral symbols that adorned the vaults and tombstones throughout the cemetery, many of which I had never seen before.) Slightly beyond there was another series of vaults and in the outer ring was a columbarium, which is a place for storing the ashes of those who have been cremated. More impressive than this was a massive, sprawling cedar tree that was older than the necropolis itself. Close by was the largest and most ornate monument in tribute to Julius Beers. It was built this large so as to block out the view of London. It was off the terrace of a church behind the cemetery and was the largest monument in the entire necropolis. Directly beneath this terrace was a catacomb of tombs sealed by a gated entrance. Even though it is sealed off to the public, many people swear they hear voices, moans, and whisperings coming from the dark depths of the tombs. (Considering that there is a tunnel that runs between the two sides of the necropolis connecting them so new arrivals or other bodies could be moved without passing through unconsecrated ground, and given that wind would be passing through the catacombs themselves, in all likelihood, what people may have been hearing was the wind, not the cries of the deceased. Still, given the environment, people can be forgiven for believing they were hearing the howls of the dead. And who am I to say some weren't?)

As I have previously stated, there have been many ghostly sightings and a large, controversial vampire scenario (which evolved into quite the circus) around Highgate. It apparently began with a pair of teenage students from La Sainte Union Convent Secondary School. As they were passing by the North gate, down Swain's Lane, they claim to have seen graves opening and bodies rising. One of the girls, by the name of Elizabeth Wojdyla, who subsequently sought help for a case of anemia (presumably due to blood loss) and nightmares about an inhuman figure hovering outside her bedroom window. The person she contacted was Sean Manchester, the famed and controversial vampire hunter who at the time was the president of the British Occult Society. (No doubt, something did give the girls a terrible fright and nightmares, but personally, I would have consulted a physician about the cause of the anemia, not a vampire hunter.)

Manchester was also contacted by a woman named Anne on behalf of her sister, who apparently had two small pin pricks in her neck and took to sleepwalking to Highgate. She was drawn to the columbarium, though how she gained entrance is a mystery. Shortly after the girls' experiences, an engaged couple was walking down the same lane when the woman suddenly let out a shriek in response to seeing what she described as some hideous being hovering behind the north gate. The fiancé turned to see what had scared her so and he, too, saw the same hideous figure. They both seemed unable to move, as though captured by this horrendous being whose face was something out of a horror movie.

Soon other reports of the sighting of this same figure emerged. It was being spoken of in local pubs and some people even went so far as to write their local papers to share their experience. To add to all of this was the discovery of animals within the necropolis drained of their blood. Things just took off from there, including a special telly feature on the program *Today*, which was to be taped in front of the north gates but a freak storm blew up, forcing them further down the lane. The remainder of the show featured Manchester on an official vampire hunt.

All of this attracted so much attention that a huge crowd showed up, trespassing all over the place. It was such a circus that the police were called in to break things up. The real topper to all this was the later discovery of a female murder victim who had been decapitated. The police strained to stifle any stories about vampires and treated it as they would many other murder cases. All in all, it was truly a mess, complete with vandalism, evidence of satanic rituals, and several arrests. The vandalized areas were cleaned up and access to the west side is severely restricted.

Manchester, with all due respect, is not taken seriously except by those deeply immersed in the occult, especially vampire lore. Nevertheless, he claimed to have exorcised and thus vanquished the Highgate Vampire, yet the stories remain very much alive and biting. The Friends of Highgate understandably deny any such vampire infestations and are extremely reluctant to even speak of the events. Vampires aside (and I again must stress that the occult, Satanism, and vampires have nothing to due with parapsychology, but I found it such an intriguing story, I could not resist including it in this volume) there have been genuine sightings of ghosts. The one I am personally familiar with is that of Rodger and Wanda. Wanda is a fashion designer and received a permit to do a fashion shoot in the West section for a couture Victorian Gothic line of apparel. During the shoot, she was tapped on the shoulder several times and turned around to see who was trying to get her attention, only to find no one there. One of the models let out a scream, pointing directly ahead of her. Everyone turned to catch a brief glance of a woman in a long black Victorian-type dress, including a veil, with her head bent and her hands clasped around her face as though she were crying. Within seconds, she vanished. This was followed by what sounded like a clap of thunder (this sound has been heard by many other people both outside and inside the necropolis). Although the sky was slightly overcast, there was no rain or thunderstorms in the forecast. Throughout the shoot, they had also been disturbed by sudden powerful gusts of wind, so strong that people were almost knocked over and the standing lights were toppled over. Before that, two of the lights blew up. These gusts of wind lasted for only seconds, then went as fast as they came. Obviously, this was rendering the shoot very difficult, not just because of the technical difficulties but the garments were being blown around so they could not be properly featured. This is in addition to the mess it made of the models' hair.

Meanwhile, after seeing the grieving woman in black, the model who first saw her got a sudden overwhelming chill and fainted. For days afterward, she was bedridden with what appeared to be flu-like symptoms except that she had no diarrhea, fever, or vomiting. She was just deathly cold and pale and so weak she could not even get out of bed to shower. All she could manage to do was shiver and sleep and it was by no means a restful sleep. Her doctor was completely baffled. Fortunately within thirteen days (lucky 13), she was fully recovered from whatever mysterious ailment befell her. This brought an end to the shoot, not only due to the model's condition and the environmental state of affairs, but because by this time, everyone was spooked, which was unusual because these are not easily frightened people. This was by no means their first graveyard shoot. They have shot in all kinds of places including castles and other graveyards. These are not superstitious people, especially Wanda. These events did get to them, though, and most of them, especially the afflicted model, vowed never to enter Highgate Cemetery again. They felt they were "trespassing" and not welcome there, permit or no permit. After relating these events to me, Wanda said that both she and Rodger had often noticed strange blue, fluent lights coming from the necropolis. It reminded them of the aurora borealis or St. Elmo's fire so it could not be mistaken for flashlights from trespassers or even the police checking out the grounds. Given the location of their home, they frequently traversed Swain's Lane. On more than one occasion they, too, heard voices around the tightly secured north gate, though it sounded more like echoes than actual people talking; they never saw any inhuman figure hovering anywhere. With that, Wanda apologized with a laugh that her house was not haunted and I graciously accepted her apology, saying that they may have better luck with their next house.

My written description of this place does not come anywhere near doing it justice. It is not only something you have to see but *experience*. I am certainly not promising you any ghostly activity, and most certainly not vampires, but for history's sake alone it is worth the trip. Otherwise, the Friends of Highgate have an official Web site that is worth checking out, as well as other sites on famous cemeteries.

Whether you visit the actual cemeteries or the Web sites, in your daily life, always remain ever vigilant to things that go bump in the night … and day! As I have pointed out many times, it can happen to anyone at any time at any place.

chapter 6
The Show Must Go On

Denny Taylor belonged to a community theatre in Windsor, Ontario. He had been hamming it up since, as he puts it, he was a kid. He joined the drama club in high school where he gained valuable educational experience in a range of areas including production, costume, lighting, and of course, acting. He truly thrived in it and on it. Everyone said that he was a natural, just born into it. He dreamed of someday making his way to the large, professional theatres and joined the local theatre group even before he graduated from high school. He loved this little theatre. It was an old, historical building. Fortunately, it had been restored after a fire in 1926 and had been carefully preserved as a historical site ever since. Perhaps due to its age and history, it had a marvelous ambience to it that is lacking in many of the newer-built theatres.

Oftentimes, before and after rehearsals, Denny would quietly sit, just soaking up the atmosphere. But on a couple of occasions, he got more than just atmosphere. In the quiet of the theatre, he swore he could hear the whispered echoes of past plays long before performed by people who had since passed on. They were the actors that had built and struggled to maintain this treasured place. At first, he thought it was simply his imagination. On one occasion following a performance, he flopped down into an overstuffed armchair that was still on stage. The place was all but empty, the audience having departed sometime before. As he was relaxing and "debriefing" as he liked to refer to reviewing the show, he heard a clear, distinct voice coming from behind him exclaiming, "Excellent performance." At first Denny thought it was one of his fellow cast members or a stagehand so he was not alarmed. The alarm came when he turned to thank the person *and there was no one there* — only vacant darkness. On another occasion, he was sitting in the front row of the theatre reading through his script. Rehearsal was not to begin for an hour and a half. This was the final rehearsal before opening night so it was quite important because the entire cast felt there were some bugs to work out. He was quite tired and fell soundly asleep. He was woken up by a tap on the shoulder and heard the word "showtime." Sure enough, the cast was just arriving. Denny rubbed his eyes, yawned and slowly turned to smile at who he thought was probably a fellow cast member or the director. Once again, there was no one there. What was there, though, was a freezing cold spot. He could almost see his breath in the air. He even moved his hand in and out of the cold spot to confirm in his mind that it was a localized phenomenon. He immediately got horripilation (the fancy medical term for gooseflesh) and darted from his seat to the stage. He had heard the odd story about the theatre being haunted but such things had never bothered or frightened him. He just didn't appreciate being spooked when he was already on edge, as he usually was before showtime.

On more than one occasion, the dark silhouette of a man could be seen sitting in the back of the theatre, sometimes in a front balcony seat, even though the place was closed. Oftentimes, during rehearsal, there would appear to be one too many people on the stage. In fact, they were not distinct figures. They appeared to be shadowy extras, which were often in areas of the stage that were not well lit. As extras were not commonly employed during rehearsal, who were these people and what were they doing on stage? The director would call for the lights to be turned up while asking these people who they were, informing them that this was a closed rehearsal. The mysterious "extras" vanished when the lights illuminated the entire stage. One figure, though, was not quite so accommodating.

During a dinner break one evening, Denny was absent-mindedly consuming a sandwich in the theatre. He chose not to go to the diner across the street with the rest of the cast. His attention was suddenly drawn away from his script to the figure of a woman, maybe in her late teens, early twenties, standing at the back of the stage (Denny was seated on the floor at the front of the stage). She was dressed in a long, turn-of-the-century dress, what Denny assumed to be a costume. She also wore a petit hat that sat slightly tilted on her head and a pair of dainty gloves. She was still and appeared rather confused as though she were either waiting for direction or pondering her environment and circumstances. Where was everyone? Why did the theatre look so different? She looked around the theatre in confusion and then down upon herself in complete dismay. She looked back out toward the direction of the audience and appeared to let out a silent cry of disbelief while burying her face in her hands, apparently crying, as Denny described it. She was in deep distress. She then slowly raised her head as though trying to compose herself and once again, stared ahead into the dark, empty audience and also, to something far beyond it. She appeared to be struggling to say something but it was as though she was mute. Denny turned to see what she could be looking at and seeing nothing, turned quickly back to the stage but the young woman was gone. Denny had heard about this mysterious figure before but this was the first time he had ever actually seen her.

As is evident, this was no vague, "shadowy figure." She was quite distinct in her appearance, and her presence had been witnessed by many others over the years. She had medium-length, blond, curly hair and large, but demure blue eyes. She was quite pretty. Interestingly, she only made her appearances when two plays were being performed. The production of *Oliver* in which she played the tragic role of Nancy, and *A Christmas Carol* in which she played the role of the Ghost of Christmas Past. This would explain in part why she always appeared in turn-of-the-century attire. She was obviously in costume. The appearance of the shadowy man sitting in the back often coincided with her appearance.

Denny, who was already interested in the paranormal, started to do some research into the history of the theatre, including those persons who had performed there in the past. Some cast members dismissed it as theatre folklore; other cast members were interested but too "freaked out" as they put it, to give it much attention. As one cast member put it, "Ignore it and it will go away." Of course that old axiom is invariably incorrect, as it certainly was in this case.

The first source of information he turned to was newspaper records. Unfortunately, they were not of much help because he was not clear on who or what he was looking for. What finally led him in the right direction was one of the nighttime janitors. (Denny didn't know why they had two janitors since the budget was so tight. He figured one of them was probably a volunteer.)

As Denny was mostly in the theatre at night, he spoke with a nighttime cleaning man by the name of Albert. He appeared to be at least in his sixties, but after inquiring, Denny learned that he was in fact seventy-two! Denny was astonished by this and asked if he was not just ready to retire and take it easy. The old gentleman replied that he would never voluntarily leave adding, "This is my home. I'll only go when they make me go! *There's always work to be finished.*"

Albert turned out to be a wealth of knowledge, having been at the theatre for so long. Denny told him about the pretty blond girl and Albert immediately knew to whom he was referring.

Her name was Laura. She was a very talented actress and, as he put it, "had the singing voice of a nightingale," adding that that name always haunted him. She was energetic, vivacious, and possessed a contagious laugh. Everyone loved her. Her father was a factory worker, as was her mother. She was the oldest of eight children. Laura wanted to pursue a career in theatre. Her mother, perhaps more practical, was firmly against this. Her father encouraged and supported her dreams. He attended every performance that she gave at the local theatre or at her high school, at least those that work permitted him to attend.

Denny further learned from this janitor that Laura believed that if she was to realize her dreams and goals, she would have to leave the small town she was living in (which in all likelihood was true). She worked part-time jobs and saved up every penny during high school to make her way to New York to start off in the small theatres there and, hopefully, make her way up. Her mother was against it but her father, not without much trepidation, maintained his support for her and her dreams. Perhaps he was remembering his own long-lost dreams he never had the opportunity to pursue.

With fearful anticipation and her usual exuberance, Laura headed off for New York and took up a room in a boarding house that was occupied with mostly aspiring young female actresses. She also landed a job as a waitress at a nearby eatery. Between the bit of money her father sent her (unbeknownst to her mother), she just made ends meet and remained optimistic and true to her dreams. She went on regular auditions and got small parts here and there. She eventually landed a role that was for her, a dream come true, and one she was completely prepared for: the Ghost of Christmas Past in *A Christmas Carol*. She considered it nothing less than a gift from God and a sign that she was on the right path. She was so grateful and excited that she could barley contain herself. The play was also in a larger, more popular theatre. Not exactly Broadway but certainly in a closer zip code! She wrote her dad and friends from her former theatre immediately. It would be the last time any of them would ever hear from her.

The show was a great success and was receiving impressive reviews. Two weeks later it was still receiving high praise, and the cast decided to go out and celebrate the success of the play. They were also having an impromptu Christmas party as it was only five days away. When the theatre would be closed for a brief period at Christmas, Laura was looking forward to going home for the holiday, especially to see her father, who had been such an unyielding support to her in spite of his concerns. Even her mother had come around a bit, but was still leery. It did appear that her dreams and vigorous work were indeed coming to fruition.

She was packed and ready to go, but she never made it home. On her way to the train station, she was raped and strangled to death.

Needless to say, her father, who had made such an effort to attend her performances and even kept a scrapbook on her, was devastated. He also felt his wife blamed him, too, even though she did not. She was just one of those who believed that "Nothing ever came from dreaming, 'less ya count heartbreak," which she so often said. He took to drinking heavily. Almost a year to the day that his daughter was murdered, he was hit by a streetcar while in a drunken stupor, dying instantly. What is most likely folklore is that in his dying breath he called out the name "Laura" (which could be heard called out faintly in the theatre). *Dead but not gone!* Albert pointed out that, as has been previously stated, her father rarely missed a performance that his daughter was in. He would always sit in the back row so as not to make her nervous. Albert was suggesting that this would account for the mysterious, shadowy figure of a man sitting in the back when no one should have been in the theatre.

Denny listened to this tragic story with a mixture of fascination and sadness, not knowing what to really believe, as theatre life is chock full of tragic stories and superstitions that can become exaggerated over time. Nevertheless, it would certainly explain many of the strange occurrences that so many actors and patrons had experienced in the old theatre: the ghostly play commentator, lights going on and off by themselves, new floodlights suddenly blowing, wind-like sounds over the PA system (calling the name Laura?), the shadowy extras, and, the most outstanding of all, the spectral actress that appeared during *A Christmas Carol* and *Oliver*. However, Denny had one more revelation yet to be revealed to him.

As Christmas was fast approaching, the cast had a rare early rehearsal of *A Christmas Carol*. Denny arrived early as usual and related the tale to the day janitor as it had been related to him earlier by the nighttime cleaner. The janitor looked at Denny with astonishment and then shook his head and smiled. Denny was confused. The janitor said, "You must be pulling my leg, young man. Albert use to be a janitor here and he would certainly be very familiar with the story of Laura and those events 'cause they took place when he worked here. But that was a long time ago and Albert passed on years ago." Then the smile faded from his face because he could not imagine how Denny could be so aware of the intricate details of the events, such as the letter Laura had sent to her father or that he had turned to drink. (For that matter, how did he know about the past janitor right down to his appearance?) None of these things had received much mention in the papers, just a short blurb about a local girl being murdered in New York and that she had performed in the theatre. It would stand to reason that the only way Denny could know so much about the tragic story of this aspiring young actress and her father was if he had actually "met" Albert, the long-deceased janitor of the theatre.

It would seem that Albert was still looking after things, Laura's father was still showing up for as many of his daughter's performances as he could, and that Laura was still showing up for performances. After all, in spite of everything, even death, *the show must go on!*

[Author's note: As the cast members and crew became accustomed to the fact that the theatre was haunted, they became quite welcoming to the two ghostly visitors. It even seemed to add some ambience to the place, and in spite of the tragic outcome of this case, they were inspired by the courage, determination, and hard work of this young woman to follow her dreams. After all, if it is truly your calling, that is the only way you are going to succeed. Denny wanted to end this chapter with a little ghost humour for you (the cast even adopted it and passed it on to friends and family), the reader. So get ready to either chuckle or roll your eyes. What happens when a ghost haunts a theatre? The actor gets stage fright.*]*

chapter 7
And Home Again:
Tony Arpa

In memory of Marianne Arpa, who died suddenly on February 23, 2008.

The days would never end it seemed, more like a dream, but reality would prove it was only an illusion. It came in like a storm and vanished like a faded memory.
~ Tony Arpa (automatic writing)

Tony Arpa in new home.

Photo by Kimberly Molto

It seems appropriate that I began this book on Merion Street and am coming full circle, ending the chapters with a further denizen of Merion Street who, like me, was in an environment where the psychic phenomena took full bloom, as it were. Tony had psychic experiences throughout his life. When I first met Tony Arpa, I knew there was something about him. He lived in the house directly across from our house; both houses were featured in Chapters 1 and 2 in my previous book, *True Tales of the Paranormal*. We both saw the Hooded Monk in our respective homes. There seemed to be a psychic umbilical cord between the two residences. At the time, neither family knew what the other family was experiencing. It just was not discussed.

Tony and I are the closest in age, and I always liked him. He was simply a positive "people person," with a generosity of spirit and a zest for life. We had much more in common than either of us realized at the time. It would be many years later when we became re-acquainted by "accident" that all these commonalities became strikingly apparent. After our meeting up again, we shared our past experiences and I interviewed him on the other events in his life since, like me, the psychic activity did not end with his moving away from Merion Street. This did not surprise me as he had strong psychic inclinations back when we knew each other, and very often employs his abilities to help, comfort, and guide others.

At the time of our reacquaintance, Tony was experiencing some health difficulties, which were nothing major. I am sorry to say that at the time of the actual recording of this interview, Tony, who had already experienced the death of his mother a few years prior, had recently lost his father to a sudden illness on July 13, 2002. That was another thing we had in common as I, too, had lost both my parents, and the current of Merion Street still ran strong through both of us. As I have said before, you can move away from Merion Street but you can never leave it.

Interview with Tony Arpa: Beginning August 29, 2002

At the time of these interviews, Tony was living in a townhouse just around the corner from my residence.

Author: It would seem appropriate to begin by reviewing some things that happened at our old haunt, Merion Street, that I was unable to cover in the first book. Can you talk about some of the events that happened to you there?

Tony: There were so many things that happened in that house I can hardly remember them all. Like things would go missing and you'd be doing something and it would turn up right in front of you. This happened to my sister once when she lost a ring and one day while she was doing the dishes, there it was, right in front of her ... out of nowhere. Another time, my mother came home to find the coffee pot taken apart (the old-fashioned percolator type) as though someone had just made a pot of coffee. She questioned all four of us about this but no one had made any coffee. She believed us and shrugged it off because she knew things like this were always happening around the house. She accepted it, even though she could not explain it, and she was psychic herself. She was not prone to speak about it; she kept it to herself.

Author: Being a devout Roman Catholic, she would not be inclined to actively engage in the spirit or psychic realm.

Tony: That's right, but I was always aware of spirits in the house. For instance, the light in the bedroom that my brother and I shared was always turning itself on and off. Once, my brother and I were sitting on the front veranda (their bedroom window overlooked the veranda) and I called to my sister, Lily, to go into the bedroom and get something for me. When she approached the bedroom door, the light switch flicked on. She called out to me and I said it wasn't me and she took off, frightened. Then, the light shut itself off.

[Author's note: I recall many summer evenings I would be on a lounging chair in the backyard writing or reading. From where I was seated, I could see the Arpa house, and my eyes would often be drawn to that bedroom light frequently going on and off. In fact, I recall thinking that those two sure go in and out of that room a lot.]

There was definitely something in that house but it was good, nothing evil or bad. It was more of a prankster. But helpful, too, like that time it let me in just as I was fumbling with my keys or my sister and her ring.

Author: There was a lot of activity around the house following your mother's death. Can you tell me about that?

Tony: Yeah. I have always been able to sense when someone is trying to reach me. The day after my mom died, I was out at her grave and I felt her presence and a physical tug on my arm. When my mom was dying, whenever I had to take her out, I told her that if she was in pain or weak, to take hold of my arm. That is what this tug felt like, like she was squeezing my arm. I said, "Ma, I know it's you. God bless ya," and then got a clear message that I should gather the family together at the house. I got hold of my sisters but couldn't reach my brother. We were waiting around outside the house as my brother Joe had the keys. The girls were getting impatient and wanted to leave but I said we couldn't. Then suddenly Joe showed up. As I hadn't been able to reach him, the timing was really weird. He had been at the lumberyard to get some material so we could make a cross for our mom's grave until a stone was placed there.

We all went into the house and Joe and I went downstairs to make the cross. As we were working on it, suddenly the room lit up as though all the bulbs were glowing beyond their capacity.

Not only that, there was light where there was not even any bulbs; an illumination. Then the lights would go dim then bright again. There was no dimmer on any of the lights. I said, "Ma, I know it's you. Can you give me another sign?" And with that, the central air came on full blast. Windows that had been locked flung open. Joe and I could hear our sisters jumping up and down upstairs. It was amazing even to me. It was a wonderful experience for all of us. We all hugged and a few tears were shed.

Author: Interesting that she selected this manner of manifestation because of a discussion you had with her when she was alive.

Tony: Yeah, because like I said, she was not prone to discussing such things, but knowing my interest in the subject she would sometimes say to me, "I know what you're reading." She asked me about what these books said about people who have passed on … what they can do to make you know they are still with you. I said they can use [manipulate] electrical currents. She asked what I meant so I explained it to her. And after she passed on, there it was; the lights, the AC.

Author: Manipulation of electromagnetic fields. No coincidence.

Tony: And the windows. When she was dying, the cancer had spread to her lungs and because she had trouble breathing, she would always be asking us to open the windows. And after she died, we would often find the windows open when no one was there to open them.

Author: Could you tell me about the incident that happened in the ICU?

Tony: I had been talking to the doctors one evening and they said she could go anytime. I couldn't sleep so I went back to the hospital and they let me in to see her. My mother asked me who the man standing beside me was. I knew she was seeing someone because when you are that close to death, doors open and you can see things others cannot perceive.

Author: Yes, there are many reports from family and medical staff of the dying pointing and saying that they see a bright horizon, an angel or a loved one.

Tony: Exactly, so I went along with it and said, "I don't know, Ma." She went on to say that he was an old man wearing a jacket with patches and that he looks poor, as though he doesn't have a thing. I suggested that maybe it was Christ trying to comfort her. Being that he was Christ he could have the world, [yet] he lived in poverty and could appear in any form. But after my mother passed away, we discovered that the gentleman buried next to her was an elderly man, and poor. He didn't have a headstone. I picked a lot of this up telepathically. Even to this day, there is just an old, worn cross and the gravesite doesn't appear as if anyone comes to see him. Not a thing or a person in the world. I'm sure of it.

Author: How eerie that he would come to her or maybe not — more of a welcoming from a lonely soul. There were other incidents following her death, as well?

Tony: One time my dad had a friend over to the house. I think she may have been a bit psychic. When my dad offered her a seat — they were in the kitchen — she said that she could not sit there. My father was very puzzled by this and asked "Why not?" She said, "Because your wife is there." Just like that. She was indicating the chair that my mother would always sit in. Another time when Joe went into the house, as he walked into the kitchen, my mom's chair was turned to face the entrance as though she was expecting a visitor, and again some of the windows were open.

[Author's note: In one of our interviews, Tony and I had a brief session using both tarot cards and a Ouija board. This interview took place in Tony's townhouse. The room this interview took place in was a combination living room/dining room. Over the dining room table where we sat was a light with a fan. The living room is off to the left of the dining room table. On the coffee table, there is a mechanical ornament that has objects that move about in a circular fashion.]

Author: In our last interview, we had a session here with the Ouija and tarot cards. Could you review what took place?

Tony: Yeah. That ornament on the table over there started to go crazy. It works on a battery and mechanical field and it just started to go wild. It was moving in all directions, really fast and wouldn't stop. *I bought that for my mother.* Before we got together, it had been operating normally. It was as if something invisible was making it move around in an erratic fashion. It had never done that before. It has settled down, but since that session, every now and then, it acts up.

Author: You stated that there were some other manifestations, as well?

Tony: Yes. Dogs are very sensitive to things like psychic phenomena. I have a ten-year-old lab. She is not afraid of anything. After that session, she hid under the dining-room table. I eventually had to coax her out. I could see she was frightened. Her tail was between her legs and her ears were down. I put her outside to calm her down. There has always been something here but after the session, there seemed to be something else; a presence or energy.

Author: We may have opened up a door or, as you have said before, these sorts of things tend to follow you around. You also stated that you had some objects fly out of the kitchen cupboard?

Tony: No. I heard glasses clanging as though someone were getting a glass for a drink. My sister and I also heard footsteps, like someone was walking around upstairs. These things happen to me wherever I've lived so I find it pretty normal. I think it will be with me until I pass on.

Author: You mentioned an event involving your father's clothes?

Tony: After my father died, I took his clothes because my dad and I were about the same size. One night I was in a deep sleep when I was suddenly woke up, not by the dog or anything, but by an overpowering presence of a person, I could feel like was the weight of a body over me. This was around 3 a.m. This presence moved over to the closet, and the door, on the left side, opened. At first, I didn't know what it meant but then I remembered that that was the side of the closet where my father's clothes were. I knew it was my dad.

Closet containing Tony's deceased father's clothes where the presence was felt and the door was flung open.

Photo by Kimberly Molto

196

This wasn't the first time he had been in the house, either. My sister Lily was visiting shortly after our dad died. We were in the backyard. There is a large, wooden fence that separates the backyards. We were talking about our dad when we both heard a resounding thud, thud, thud from the wooden fence. I went around the back of the fence to see if it was the neighbours but there was no one there. Both Lily and I knew it was a sign from our dad. While he was alive, he had never been over to see my house. He always promised me that he would come over but never made it for one reason or the other, but after his death, he did give me these signs.

Author: So he kept his promise to come and see your new house. In your case, you've had so many things happen to you over the years you just take it for granted.

Tony: So many it's hard to remember them all.

Author: You try to use these gifts to help others, as well?

Tony: Whenever I can. Like just six months ago, a troubled young man came to see me 'cause he heard I did readings. I knew nothing of his future plans but in the reading I saw two possible outcomes. One positive and the other was death by his own hand. This took him back because he had never mentioned suicide to anyone. I tried my best to dissuade him from this, assuring him that he would be going through a rough patch, but if he only rode it out, as tough as that may be, things would turn out good. A few months later, after his proposal of marriage was turned down, he killed himself. I guess that, on top of everything else, was too much.

Author: When death is revealed, it is a very problematic situation. If it is unavoidable, like a terminal illness or heart attack, do you tell or not? One would hope that we all are aware that when we get up in the morning, we have no way of knowing if this is our last day here or not. On the other hand if it is suicide, all you can do is try to dissuade them, offer them hope and give them a glimpse at the light at the end of the tunnel.

Tony: Exactly. You can't control people's destiny or actions. Sometimes I wonder if this is a gift or a curse because sometimes you can make a difference and help, which is great but other times, you see it and there is nothing you can do. That doesn't feel so good. But in the end, I think it's all from God, so it's good.

Auther: Thank you for your time, Tony. I know we'll be speaking soon.

Tony: No problem. I'll be looking forward to it.

When I asked Tony what he thought about this particular part of Merion Street, why it was such a hot zone of psychic activity, he postured what I had already speculated. It is some sort of a vortex. This was later confirmed by two psychics, Madeline and Julian, adding that there is a triangle of energy ranging from the middle part of the road crossing to connect the two houses that were the former residences of Tony and I. Madeline made note of this in 2002 and Julian in 2007; neither had any prior knowledge of the locations of the two houses. Electromagnetic fields converge and attract activity and spirits that may never have had any connection with that area. These areas can shift as the one of the houses appears to have been quiet for sometime now.

The house written about in Chapter 1 is farther down the street. Even walking down the street, friends have commented that it feels "spooky." With the writing of this chapter, a number of unusual occurrences have taken place for Tony. First, we had another shared experience, this time involving telephones. As you read in Chapter 1, I received incoming calls from Merion Street while I was at the actual residence.

One time Tony received a phone call, which in and of itself is not unusual save for one thing: the incoming phone call was *from Tony*. On another occasion, Tony's brother had stopped by for a visit and when he got home, there was a message from Tony. How could this be possible?

Tony was visiting with his brother at the time the call was placed so he certainly would not have called his brother at home.

Also, many anomalous events took place during not only the writing of this book but the two Merion Street chapters in particular. In fact, at one point, this chapter was so mangled (even the letters were in bold red) that it was pulled from the book. Being unhappy with this, I gave the chapter another shot. Some of the material had to be transcribed directly from the audio tapes. At one point, the tape recorder flew right off the table, landing several metres from the desk. I immediately rang Tony and after pressing the first two numbers, the phone dialed itself and *not much to my surprise,* the voice on the other end was none other than Tony (I do not have him on speed-dial).

Shortly thereafter, while writing about the death of his mother, the light over the computer went on and off, finally staying off. I checked the cords and the bulb but nothing was amiss. As you previously read, Mrs. Arpa was a strict Catholic, not prone to discussing such things. Perhaps she did not want it discussed in a book, either. I then sat back and asked her if she would prefer that I not include her or this chapter in the book. The light immediately came back on. I took that for an approval. There is also a rosary hanging over the light; it occasionally swings gently as though she is watching over the chapter … or my shoulder.

During the final edit, the beads once again began to swing, but this time I felt a slight pressure on my right shoulder. Coincidently, I often feel the urge to call Tony at these times but tend to put it off until later. Could this also be Mrs. Arpa looking out for her children as of the writing of this chapter? Tony is experiencing some health problems. Notes and other things would continually fly off the desk. At times I would be working on another chapter when the rosary and light would act up and the Arpa chapter would suddenly pop up. I would call Tony at these times and sure enough, he was in a very bad way. The computer itself developed a mind of its own. *It would not keep the selected formatting. Paragraphs would split in two leaving half a page blank. The chapter was becoming mangled again.*

There was not a thing I could do to control it. I simply had to merge paragraphs as best I could. I can only hope it keeps its designated format. One of the strangest things of all is that in reconstructing the chapter, I had to refer to the audio tapes. At the conclusion of the last interview, I heard the click where I had turned the tape recorder off but the tape itself was still running as I was transcribing. A couple of seconds later, the well-known theme from the movie *Halloween* began to play! I got chills. Where did that come from and why? Merion Street lives on ...

Though this is the end of the chapter, it is hardly the end of the story, but I will leave the last words of this chapter to Tony, which he received through automatic writing:

Take a Look
Can you see the cities, standing very tall?
Can you see the people surrounded by these walls?
Take a look, can you see,
Is man as free as he can be?
Can you see the fury in our desert streets?
Are the people fighting or are they out to compete?
Take a look, can you see?
Is man a wanderer, is he free?
Can you see the sky; is it still your favorite colour?
Will man destroy it or will he leave it for another?
Take a look, can you see,

Is man forever in need of me?
Can you feel the world turn; it spins like a top.
Will man's ignorance make it someday stop?
Take a look my people and someday you'll understand,
You were created in my image but never to command.
~ *circa* 1976, Merion Street

appendix
Ghostbusters: Quantum
Quarks in a Brave New World

In my previous book, *True Tales of the Paranormal*, I dedicated a chapter to some of the scientific theories that may apply to the mechanics of some types of psychic phenomena (PSI=φ). This appendix will only offer up a brief synopsis as there are so many books and papers that deal with nothing but the scientific aspect of this fascinating field, written by persons much more qualified than myself. These include mathematicians, physicists, experts in electrodynamic conduction and fields, MDs, psychologists, and others who are considered true investigators of parapsychology like Scott Rogo, Raymond Bayless, William Roll (who has put more time in researching poltergeists in recent times than anyone else), J.B. Rhine, Dr. Karlosis Osis, Raymond Moody, and Edgar Mitchell (to name just a few in a long list) who have dedicated their lives and in some cases even established research institutes or departments within universities dedicated to the study of PSI, i.e., ESP/telepathy, near-death experiences, reincarnation, etc. Terms and words that you have probably already become familiar with in other books on the paranormal, as well as those you will be coming across more and more in the near future are explained here and in the glossary. For a thorough read on the scientific aspects, there are many excellent books and articles focusing on those specific topics at libraries and on the Internet. Even if they are older, do not be put off, as they have stood the test of time. By the time this book hits the shelves, there will be new papers and books as the advancements and discoveries march on.

Part One
Quirky Quantum, Reality, and PSI

While reviewing and condensing the physics and mathematics for this part of the book I was constantly reminded of a line from a Pink Floyd album, "For I've looked over Jordan and I've seen, things are not what they seem." As advancements and discoveries progress in science, the underlying structure of reality, including what we see on a day-to-day basis, is not what it seems.

Whenever I read up on theoretical physics and applied mathematical formulations, whether related to PSI or not, I am in awe. It has given me a new perception of the universe and world we live in, as well as a better understanding of anomalous events that I have been documenting and researching for over two decades. It has also given me and many others pause as we realize that we need to take a second, good hard look at what we call the reality. I suppose in time a lot of those things we do not yet understand will later be taken for granted, like gravity and that the world is round and not flat, but to get to that point we require more research.

As a result of all the research and my own personal experiences, I was sure of the authenticity of PSI events but was confused as to why all but such a minute part of the scientific community did not seem interested. Conventional science has not invested a lot of time and money into researching parapsychology (or what I like to call para-physics and if there is no such word, there is now) for a number of reasons, including the problematic factor that PSI tends to be intangible, unpredictable, and for the most part, uncontrollable. This renders the study of PSI especially challenging. It is not something that can be collected, packed up in a box or test tubes and brought back to a lab where it can be studied in a controlled environment. Nor can it be summoned up on demand or contained once present. Furthermore in science, testing a theory or hypothesis must be repeated, which is obviously problematic with PSI phenomena. Even working with those individuals where it has been established that they are the authentic thing, i.e. people who possess "something" like ESP or telekinesis; they are humans, not machines or lab rats, nor are they magicians who can perform on demand. This is as frustrating to the psychics (or test subjects) as it is to the scientists.

Combined with these challenges and obstacles is research funding, which is a major concern in all areas of science. Whether it is government, private sector, or corporate support, a business degree often appears to be more fitting than a PhD or MD, as you have to spend so much time presenting the cost/benefit ratio and projected financial profits. I recall more than one of my former professors commenting that they spent more time in boardrooms than labs! (I must interject here that most scientists do not make the best business persons. Conversely, most MBAs do not make the greatest scientists and in a lab are akin to a bull in a china shop.) Especially in the private sector, a presentation is required to demonstrate the projected outcomes, how it is applicable, and what the return on the investment will be. The enlightenment, advancement of human understanding of our world/universe or the possible overall benefits to humankind is of little or no interest to the corporate sector, and the government has other more pressing concerns.

If this funding criteria was in place back in the "good old days.," we would not have such inventions as the laser. At the time, those who discovered and developed this magnificent technology did not fully comprehend what its applications could be, so it required more research funding to further refine it and thus ascertain its potential uses (the same applied to insulin). Now look at the many and varied applications of the laser and the lives saved by insulin. Commercial applications or value often do not become apparent until after the facts have been established. Therefore a large body of the funding is derived from donations, bequests, memberships, and the money generated from the work of established organizations dedicated to PSI research, including departments in various universities.

I have gone off on a bit of a rant here but with the inherent problems researching PSI and the funding difficulties, I felt it necessary to explain why a large part of the scientific community is not jumping at some of these fascinating phenomena. I should add that many scientists just don't see the connection or even accept the validity of PSI activity.

John Polkinghorne of the Department of Applied Mathematics and Theoretical Physics at Cambridge University once stated that, "Your average quantum mechanic is about as philosophically minded as your average car mechanic."[1] Those that do at least accept not only the possibility but the probability of it are afraid for their careers and reputations. Even I was warned that publishing books of this nature could affect my chances of receiving grants in the future for "serious research." This is nothing new. In fact it dates back to the nineteenth century (where in some cases the critics became converts and joined forces to form The American and British Society for Psychical Research and forged on with their research and publishing). Author Catherine Crowe wrote in the preface of her collection of ghost stories that, "I avow, that in writing this book, I have a higher aim than merely to afford amusements ... I wish to engage the attention of my readers, because I am satisfied that the opinions (that I am advocating), if seriously entertained, would produce very beneficial results."

Thankfully, a growing number of scientists are not overly concerned with matters of reputation and are pursuing such research and are willing to share their findings with those who specialize in paranormality. Thank heavens for that and for those dedicated individuals and organizations that are pursuing it because they are revealing what a truly fascinating, wonderful, and wild world we live in, much like Alice's Wonderland.

Let's begin with some terms that if you have not yet encountered while reading books on the paranormal, you will: quantum vacuum and hologram, zero point field, virtual particles, and the space/time continuum (believe me, there are many more) and how they may relate to or help us understand PSI. (My background is actually in cognitive-neurobiology and altered states of consciousness, so no doubt the experts in applied mathematics and quantum/theoretical physics will be rolling their eyes at parts of my evaluation and translation of these complex and specialized fields, but I can't let that stop me. In fact I would more than welcome their feedback for clarification!

It is well established that everything, from coffee tables to the air we breathe, our bodies and minds as well as the very thoughts we produce to the universe in general, is composed of energy, albeit existing at different frequencies, forms, and amplitudes (energy output). It is also well established that energy does not die; it changes form. We are surrounded and bombarded by this energy in many forms both natural and man-made, i.e., radio and some electromagnetic waves. We, ourselves, generate and emit such fields. Certainly our brains produce electrical currents as can be demonstrated daily in a well-known diagnostic procedure known as an EEG. These conditions have been investigated in relation to telepathy (harmonizing with the electrical frequency output of another individual no matter the distance) and as a possible explanation for auras that many people assert that they can see. (Recall in cases in which people have died then were revived, encountering living multicoloured lights that were like consciousness, oftentimes communicating with them.) Without launching into a dissertation on quantum mechanics, applied physics, and particles both virtual and nonvirtual, I will move on to the stuff of the universe, reality, and consciousness.

Part Two
Is All We See But a Dream Within a Hologram ...

My revision on Poe's famous line came about as a result of my researching what is known as the Quantum Hologram, which was discovered by the German mathematician, Dr. Walter Schempp, *circa* 1992. In effect it explores four basic quantum processes that are comprised of entanglement, coherence/quantum correlation, and the two I have focused on in relation to PSI, nonlocality and interconnectedness.

Nonlinear and nonlocality (near and far) in and of themselves change our perception of reality. In PSI there are anomalous events in which a person or object can be in two places at the same time, such as bilocation, and to a lesser degree, phantoms of the living and astral projection. We are not accustomed to this, which is why it is referred to as an anomalous event. The same applies to the nonlinear concept. We expect point A to lead to point B. This is not necessarily the case in the quantum world or hologram. To quote the eminent scientist Edgar Mitchell (former Apollo 14 astronaut), "The omnipresent and omni-directional transfer of influence (including thought, emotion and interaction) at the quantum level instantly, simultaneously and ubiquitously, through a wave-like or field-like resonance wherein spatial and temporal factors are *inconsequential.*"

He further goes on to say that, "The state of a universe that is considered to be unified and joined together holistically, through a process of non-local resonance occurring within the underlying zero-point field [more of that to come] that *connects all matter, energy and information in the cosmos.*"[2] This is the emergence of the physics of the twenty-first century where physicists are echoing ancient wisdom and teachings (such as the Akashic Records: see glossary for further details). These emerging theories are a dramatic paradigm shift altering our perception and understanding of realty, existence, life, and even death.

When physicists speak, albeit in technical terms, of all thoughts, emotions, and energy being permanently recorded in the "ethers," they are saying things that are strikingly similar to what the ancient mystics, philosophers, and psychics have been saying for eons. We leave our imprints or footsteps in the ethereal sands of time and space (so watch where you step). Time and space itself is also being reconsidered because of the theory of the space/time continuum and the multi-universe. If we combine nonlocality, nonlinear, and the multi-universe theories with the discovery of the zero point field, then PSI phenomena becomes to look quite logical, not crazy. (Since this is the second time I mentioned it, a definition of the zero point field is due.) It is thus named because fluctuations in the field exist within a temperature of absolute zero degree of Kelvin, where all matter has been removed. Particles continually interact with the underlying zero point field by virtual particles. The latter continually appear out of the quantum vacuum (which possesses an elaborate structure), combining and wiping each other out within seconds. Virtual particles are so named because they have such a brief life span that they are virtually non-existent. How is that is for a paradox: they exist but not really, yet they carry a vital influence. All matter, including that which we can see, not see or sense (which would logically include ghosts, which are ethereal matter/energy) is supported and sustained from within the underlying zero point field. *This field is a depository of all fields and all ground energy states for the different forces in nature, and all the virtual particles, which mediate these forces.*

If your eyes have not yet glazed over or crossed, I will simply add that space itself at the level of the quantum vacuum is a playground fully packed with energy and particles, *which provides the platform for physical manifestation, which logically would include psychic manifestations.* The physicist P. Davies echoes the language of the mystics and psychics when he speaks of the quantum ether, and H.P. Blavatsky elaborates on these theories stating that, "Space itself, not the underlying space/time complex, but the underlying 'Eternal Parent Space' with its 'ceaseless breath' or movement, is the foundation for all physical manifestation (as stated above). The Zero point field is similarly an ether, the invisible foundation for physical manifestation." It not only has the tone of spiritualism but theology as well, even God, but that is a whole other subject I will not pursue here.

In his book *Beyond the Quantum: God, Reality, Consciousness in the New Scientific Revolution*, Michael Talbot even has an entire chapter entitled "Mathematical Evidence for the Existence of God;" he is not the only author to pursue this line of thinking. I had briefly touched on the time/space continuum. Marie D. Jones phrased it up nicely by sating that, "We know that at the quantum level (time) is not linear, and that the past, present, and future all exist at once. For every now we experience, a positive wave flows into the future and a negative wave flows into the past not unlike the ripple effect created by dropping a pebble into the water." This has implications for pre/retrocognition, telepathy, ESP, and premonitions.

In a multidimensional universe, there exists a multitude of possible outcomes so most premonitions or predictions cannot be absolute or precise, especially when you include not only the physics but personal, human bias that is unavoidable in many cases. Even physicists have not found many true physical absolutes. It also resonates with the ancient law of karma and in Christianity's "what you sow so shall ye reap," and in general, the cause and effect principle but again, in the quantum world, this is not always due to the unpredictable and multiple variables. Do you recall the rather paradoxical Newtonian theory that for every action there is an equal and opposite reaction? Most of us have had experiences that we have done everything we were so suppose to do and it came out wrong or we achieved the opposite of what we were striving for.

What happened? Déjà vu is another common experience that can be related to the time/space continuum, only are we tapping into the past or the future? Again, there are few true absolutes, which also raises some interesting questions about fate and destiny. I recall attending a lecture by a theoretical physicist and even though I took notes throughout his fascinating lecture, something he said that stuck with me and further inspired me to continue with my research and investigation into mathematics and physics and the paranormal. I may be paraphrasing a tad but he essentially stated that, "We generate electromagnetic fields by our thought processes and our biological activity and many of these [haunted houses] are constructed of materials that are easily magnetized, such as brick for example, which contains various salts and silica, the same thing you find in recording tape. These imprints are scanned directly in to the physical structure and that the person whose brain is especially sensitive to these fields ... it's possible that their brains could act as a VCR and decode this recorded material." This theory has been covered in a couple of chapters of this book and is speculated to be the cause of so-called residual ghosts (those hauntings that are like recordings caught in a feedback loop and are activated when the necessary elements converge both environmental and the human element).

For those not familiar with the scientific theories being considered and applied to paranormal, I have condensed and thrown a lot at you, but trust me when I say that I have not even scratched the surface. Yet even in this brief, sketchy overview, that common opinion that those who have experienced anomalous events or those who claim to have psychic abilities are crazy or under the influence of drugs or alcohol does not hold up. In fact, the question turns from "how can such things exist?" to "how can such things NOT exist?" Other theories that I explored in my previous book and which have been more elaborately covered in other books and papers include decision augmentation, teleological model of PSI, the model for pragmatic information, and many more electromagnetic, neurological and quantum/mathematical theories.

For those truly interested in the science related to PSI, I hope the little I have presented inspires you to read more on the subject as there are volumes of it and it does not merely apply to PSI. It is applicable to our daily lives and how we perceive reality. If zero point fields, quantum vacuums, multi-universe/dimensions, and the rest of the terminology does not click with you, just remember what they represent; points to ponder, as it were. Our thoughts, emotions, dreams, and actions leave permanent imprints that can have consequences and be tapped into. They are stored in the "ether" (zero point field). Energy does not die, it changes form. Time is not necessarily linear and energy in whatever form is not necessarily localized. Though it is often referred to as twenty-first-century physics, much of this is ancient. Just the language has changed. The absence of proof is not the proof of absence.

Part Three
Who You Gonna Call? Ghostbusters, Ghosts, and Entities: Things That Go Bump in the Lab

Please note that there is a difference in a straight field investigation where the purpose, if all goes well, can be establish as to whether or not there is actual paranormal activity. Other groups or individuals go beyond that with the goal being to "cleanse, bless or actually exorcise" the troublesome manifestation.

During our investigations, we often map out the environment in an almost forensic pattern. (Incidentally, when we consult with a psychiatrist it has nothing to do with mental instability but is employed because some people with certain afflictions are more prone or susceptible to some types of PSI phenomena like non-psychotic depression and certain types of migraine and epilepsy. They also tend to be artistic, introspective, and empathetic, often times overly so.) This would suggest a possible neurological susceptibility, which has already been investigated. (The Canadian neurosurgeon, Wilder Penfield, went so far as to say that if there is a seat of the soul it is located in the right temporal lobe, also associated with telepathy and ESP.)

Whether or not there is PSI activity, the human element cannot be ignored. We do engage in spiritual release, as you have read in this book. That is when a spirit is "trapped" by tragic circumstances and cannot move on (as happens to the living, as well). In other cases, for some reason, the deceased does not know they are dead, whether out of shock, disbelief, or as one psychic put, displacement syndrome, and consider the inhabitants the interlopers who should be banished. There are also cases where the death was a sudden, tragic accident or a suicide where the spirit is in shock or regret/guilt and is a lost "mournful soul." We do subscribe to belief in malevolent spirits who were, upon investigation, malevolent in life. However, we are not especially scholarly or experienced on "demons" or "possessions." In such cases, a referral would be made if that was the request of the expedients. I am not stating these as facts; they are theories we, as well as others, have developed and work with until we learn more. Much is being made of such equipment as ion detectors, electromagnetic field detectors (EMF), Geiger counters (if there is Radon gas or any radiation that might not only be the cause of the manifestations, i.e. hallucinations, but they have a more serious and immediate problem than PSI activity, then their use would only be as an instrument of elimination). ORBs have received much attention as well, perhaps too much as they can simply be condensation, an insect, dust, or a normal anomaly related to the film, just as happens with X-ray films on occasion. Some cameras are even being made with special filters to eliminate this problem.

Obviously, if you are using such a camera and a solid mist or ORB is present along with other anomalies such as a localized cold spot or drop in overall room temperature, you may have something more than a dust particle. Whatever the case may be, you must be acutely aware of the environment, including what material the house or environment contains (including outdoors).

When investigating a poltergeist case, we found it not only vital to get to know the people involved, the psychological dynamics of the person(s) but then proceed to get to know the poltergeist, as funny as that may sound. I am aware that there are those that believe a poltergeist is a disembodied, mischievous spirit, which always struck me as being nonsensical and a waste of energy but, with all due respect, from my own personal experiences with poltergeist activity combined with years of investigating them, I have been led to a different conclusion, which is not to say I am correct. Perhaps both schools of thought are correct, depending on the case. In getting to know the poltergeist I needed to determine if there were any repeated patterns, targets, and what the target trajectory, is if any. That is where the forensics first came in; like mapping out a crime scene and deciphering the clues. This proved to be a very helpful technique. We were looking for the target(s) to determine if there was an emotional or psychological component associated with the activity, i.e. objects, belonging to a fellow family member or the poltergeist agent themselves; sentimental objects that belonged to a lost loved one, an object of frustration (like a computer) and so on. Or if it is random and the objects are not associated with any elemental psychological associations, such a case would suggest a psychic outburst of repressed energy. Along those same lines the trajectory is used to determine if there is a target being aimed at or avoided so as to prevent harm or breakage or visa versa. Obviously, if it is aimed at a person or object, that is a target. If it is haphazard, there may still be an object of frustration, anger, grief, etc., but it is considered a psychic paroxysm where the internal damn has burst or sprung a leak. In cases where an individual is identified as the source of the poltergeist, we can then turn our attention to the underlying cause of the outbursts and guide the individual in the use of techniques proven to assist in harnessing, channeling, and redirecting the energy in a more constructive way as opposed to the messy and expensive (and it can be costly!) poltergeist. Of course if the poltergeist is a result of psychological or physical trauma, referrals are made whether requested or not. In yet other cases, there is an underlying physical problem not yet diagnosed or unresolved emotional issues, i.e. grief, anger, etc.

We, as well as many others, have found equipment to be of limited value in the case of poltergeists due to the underlying nature of it being an elusive little devil and a (self) saboteur. It also seems to be camera- and witness-shy, which adds to the frustration of the experiencer, since it does happen, but not in front of anyone, as though on purpose. Video cameras would have to be on continuous record mode and set up in every room of the residence, which is impractical, not to mention an invasion of privacy in some obvious places. Nevertheless, that does not preclude their use altogether (until the camera becomes one of the targets, which has happened). A further problem is that unlike a ghost or haunted house, what we are dealing with in this case is a *haunted person*. Therefore the activity is not localized, thus it can take place anywhere and at anytime. EMF detectors share similar problems. They are useful but will register a spike that can be the result of a sudden jerky movement by the person holding the equipment (and who wouldn't jump?) or from the individual themselves. However, if there is a sudden spike, it could be an indication that something may be about to occur, which is a good heads up. Poltergeists are also quick and all over the place, nor do they follow a fixed schedule, which further complicates the use of EMF detectors unless the activity only takes place in areas where there is a source of electrical energy or even overhead power lines across the residence that boost the internal psychic energy of the individual. That requires a differential diagnosis, i.e. baseline reading, against those things when the poltergeist agent is present. Our best outcomes have always been those protocols described above and working with the individual themselves.

Both Chris Howard and I can personally attest to this as we have both experienced poltergeist activity. The one mystery we have yet to resolve, which is not always related strictly to poltergeist cases, is the materialization of objects known as aports. In the case of poltergeists, things generally disappear or break. "Presents" are a nice turn of events but are more often associated with hauntings. Other types of aports specially associated with poltergeists are pebbles or small stones falling from what appears to be midair. Puddles of water are also common with poltergeist activity and water is not only electrically charged and packed with ions but is an apparent conductive element in PSI activity. Thus, as I have pointed out before, the well-worn "it was a dark and stormy night" line has a tangible and physical basis. (The house my family lived in back in the 1970s was the perfect environment for PSI activity as it was constructed primarily of limestone; we later discovered that it has an underground water reservoir and was built atop a huge, obviously submerged boulder. It was in this house that PSI activity exploded for me and awakened my own psychic abilities as well as a couple of other family members.)

Contact with the deceased and visa versa has been going on for eons. In the twentieth century, Thomas Edison even ventured into it, telling a reporter for *Scientific American* that he had developed a machine that could indeed be used to contact the dead. He later made light of this but, no doubt, he was quite serious. It only makes sense that spirits would access our vast array of electronic gadgets to communicate with us. I would surmise that being that they are in pure energy form as opposed to corporeal it might be easier for them to reach us via electronic equipment than to tap us on the shoulder, write on a fogged up mirror or materialize in full body form.

All science aside, what is truly relevant to people is the experience they have had, what it meant to them, and what effect it had on their lives. They are not overly concerned with whether or not science accepts it or can offer up theories or explanations any more than people who believe in a God, regardless of their religious affiliation or lack of one, require any scientific proof. In fact, while explaining some of the physical theories being considered to understand PSI, one woman who had had contact with her deceased son told me about a cartoon in which a cleaning lady was vacuuming up a mess in a physics lab, shaking her head muttering, "Particles! Particles!" The woman telling the story added, "Particles, smarticles! What do I care? I was blessed and comforted by a visit from my son. I saw and heard him. I know he is at peace, which is all that matters to me. I am that cleaning woman who lives in the real not virtual world, that cleans the lab coats of the scientists trying to prove or disprove it or understand it. It is what it is and that's enough for me." Particles, schmarticles? What else can I say? That pretty much sums it up for those people whose lives have been touched and changed by a brush with the paranormal. I respect that immensely but also appreciate and understand the need for continued scientific research, as well.

Notes

Chapter 2

1. Viktor E. Frankl, *Man's Search for Meaning* (New York: Pocket Books, 1959), 121.
2. Viktor E. Frankl, *Man's Search for Meaning* (New York: Pocket Books, 1959), 176.

Chapter 5

1. Rosemary Ellen Guiley, *The Encyclopedia of Ghosts and Spirits, Third Edition* (New York: Facts on File, 2007), 203.

Appendix — Ghostbusters: Quantum Quarks in a Brave New World

1. John C. Polkinghorne, *The Quantum World* (Harlow, UK: Longman, 1984).
2. Dr. Edgar Mitchell, "What is the Quantum Hologram?" article, Quantum Hologram FAQ, http://www.edmitchellapollo14.com/QHFAQs.htm.

* Also see the National Institute for Discovery Science: "Nature's Mind: the Quantum Hologram." Edgar Mitchell, PhD www.nidsci.org/articles/mitchell_hologram.php.

Glossary

Akashic Records: The term for what is believed to be the permanent record of all thoughts, emotions, and deeds throughout history and recorded in the Universal Mind, Cosmic Consciousness, or Mind of God. It is believed that in altered states of consciousness, one is able to gain access to this universal pool of consciousness. It has also been suggested that this is the means by which artists or scientists get their ingenious inspirations. There are similar ideas in most of the world's religions and mysticism, e.g. the God in Christianity is thought to have a book of records (though not literally) where each individual's thoughts and actions (including the effect they have on the lives of others) is recorded. According to those who have died and been revived, all these things are reviewed. In physics, this pool of consciousness is hypothetically associated with the zero point field (written about in Appendix A), sometimes referred to as the ether, i.e. hypothetical field, thought to pervade all space and time and to be the conduit through which electromagnetic waves are generated and where all activity is stored and manifests from.

Electronic Voice Phenomena (EVPs): Voices on an audio tape that should not be there. They are often thought to be the voices of the dead and in some cases, may be but many such tapes have been shown to have picked up random radio frequencies, even cell phones, or break through voices from a previous recording if it is a used tape. There are computer programs that can isolate and enhance audio, video, and still photographic impressions, though they are not one hundred percent. Still, they are very worthwhile.

Hyperesthesia: An extraordinary acute sensory awareness.

ORBs: Unexplained, usually singular white or blue areas in a developed picture are present. Often, especially in recent times interpreted as being evidence of the presence of a spirit or entity; however, under further investigation, the cause is often found to be light reflections from the flash or light bulb, insects, dust particles, camera strap or moisture on the lens (in recent times, there have been cameras developed to filter out these ORB effects). This is not always the case, so there are a number ORBs that remain of undetermined cause or origin. One must be keenly aware of their environment while shooting a picture, which most of us are not unless we are actively engaged in an investigation. If the occurrence is accompanied by other phenomena such as cold spots, lights blowing, etc., this would certainty support a paranormal manifestation. There are also rare photos that have been taken where a red streak cuts through the picture and one of the persons being photographed falls ill or worse. Still other even rarer photos have been taken when someone was present when the photo was taken but were not there upon development. They had evidently not been cut off. In again rare cases, these "missing" individuals later died. Yet another rare occurrence is the appearance of a (usually but not always) deceased person not physically present when the photo was taken. ORBs should not be mistaken for "spirit photography" where the image of a person, known or unknown, appears on the developed film. A careful analysis must be conducted to eliminate such things as double exposure. Always hold on to the negatives, original photo or CD-ROM.

Quantum Field Theory: A physical field considered as a collection of particles and forces and observable properties of an interacting system, which are expressed as finite quantities rather than as state vectors. (Vector = a physical quantity that has both magnitude and direction.)

Quantum Vacuum: Being devoid of any form of matter. The space housing an infinite sea of electrons having negative energy, which is observed as being empty space.

Retrocognition/precognition/premonitions: I have combined these three in the same category because although they differ they are also interrelated and sometimes occur in combination with one or the other. If you recall from Appendix A, time is a continuum that has a ripple effect. Present activity simultaneously flows into the past and the future. That is, in part, problems and reasons with foretelling the future; there are very few absolute certainties due to the many variable factors (including so-called divine intervention), which cannot be known so the closest one could come is the most probable outcome. (Such is the case where a woman had been trying to become pregnant and went to see a psychic out of fun. She was indeed pregnant with a boy, both of which were verified later by her doctor; however, the psychic saw no baby in the near future. As it turned out, the infant was stillborn. Note that the focus was on her pregnancy and gender of the baby, not the outcome.) RETROCOGNITION is the deliberate or involuntary act of tuning into past events of which the recipient has no practical way of knowing or no previous knowledge of. Sometimes this is done by merely entering the space where the event took place, touching an object that has the stored energy of a person (psychometry) or the event. PRECOGNITION is the ability to see events in the future. This can also be deliberate or an "accident" experienced by a hypersensitive individual who tunes into a person or an event related to something that has caught their interest. In both cases there are often actual physical symptoms such as chills or a mild flushing or headache. It is also accompanied by an overwhelming "gut feeling" of certainty that they cannot shake. A PREMONITION is more frequent than is probably reported until after the event. It is spontaneous and frequently occurs when a person is in a slightly altered state of consciousnesses, such as doing something repetitive like long-distance driving, knitting, etc., where a person is almost in an hypnotic state or the neurological state one is in prior to falling asleep or waking up (hypnagogic/hypnopompic). Although they are very clear and real to the experiencer, so much so that they may change their plans as a result of the *vision,* they are often not recognized until after the event foreseen has taken place. (I would suggest writing such visions down, dating them, and keeping them in a sealed envelope. This was actually the case in one family, in which a mother foresaw the death of her son. The daughter made note of it. He was prompted to change his plans as his mother had "the second sight," which the family respected, and also to put his mother's mind at ease. The train he was to take did derail, with a few dead and many injured.)

There are also very well-known premonitions related to events such as the *Titanic* in which people cancelled their reservations. (I thought I had heard all the stories related to people foreseeing this tragedy, but a very unique one with a couple of interesting twists was recently related to me.)*

* The following account was related to me by an elderly British lady who I have known for years named Marian. She would often regale me with stories such as surviving the bombing blitz over England and the like. We happened upon the topic of premonitions and the *Titanic*. It has qualities of both being a premonition and precognition. The events happened to a writer by the name of W.T. Stead, who, as a boy, suffered from recurring nightmares of an ocean liner colliding with an iceberg and sinking. He had no explanation for these bizarre nightmares. They left such a strong impression on him that when he grew up, he wrote a story entitled "From the Old World to the New" that featured the ocean liner from his nightmares, which sank after hitting an iceberg. He named his vessel the *Majestic* and its captain E.J. Smith. Twenty years following the publication of his story, he accepted an invitation to be a guest speaker at a lecture in the United States. The

Vertical Dream: A dream in which the content centres around true life events, which the dreamer has no knowledge of, whether it be centred on the past, present, or future. The dreams can be familiar or unrelated to the dreamer.

Vertical Impression: Knowledge that is imparted on an individual without their conscious awareness. Its source can be multitudinous, such as a spirit guide, a deceased love one, or an unknown person. Often inspirational.

Xenoglossy: The expression of foreign communication either spoken or written that is not known to the experiencer, including dead languages like Latin and Aramaic.

---

vessel he boarded was the RMS *Titanic*. He never made it to New York, as he was one of the many that went down with the "unsinkable ship." In keeping with the tradition that a captain goes down with his ship, one of the other persons to die was the captain of the *Titanic*. His name was E.J. Smith, the "fictional" captain of the *Majestic* from a twenty-year-old story.

Other Books by Kimberly Molto

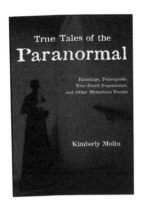

True Tales of the Paranormal
Hauntings, Poltergeists, Near-Death Experiences,
and Other Mysterious Events
978-1-55002-410-4
$22.99

This intriguing examination of reincarnation, premonitions, and other spooky inexplicables from a scientific perspective explores modern scientific theories and current research. The author also provides suggestions on how to deal with paranormal experiences and where to go for help and information.

Of Related Interest

The Big Book of Canadian Ghost Stories
John Robert Colombo
978-1-55002-844-7
$29.99

By Canada's Mr. Mystery, more than 175 accounts of haunted houses, ghosts and poltergeists, weird visions, and assurances of life after death are told by the witnesses themselves. Whatever your views are about the supernatural and the paranormal — skeptic, believer, middle-of-the-road — this huge collection of stories filled with thrills and chills will cause you to wonder about the nature of human life and the afterlife.

Strange But True
John Robert Colombo
978-1-55002-735-8
$22.99

Shake hands with your fears and dreads. Here are engrossing and unsettling occurrences that are supernatural or psychical, paranormal or parapsychological, all between the covers of one book. Not for the faint of heart! These fascinating first-person accounts originated in the columns of old newspapers or in the highly readable narratives derived from correspondence conducted by the author with present-day witnesses.

Available at your favourite bookseller

 **DUNDURN PRESS**
www.dundurn.com

Tell us your story! What did you think of this book? Join the conversation at
www.definingcanada.ca/tell-us-your-story by telling us what you think.